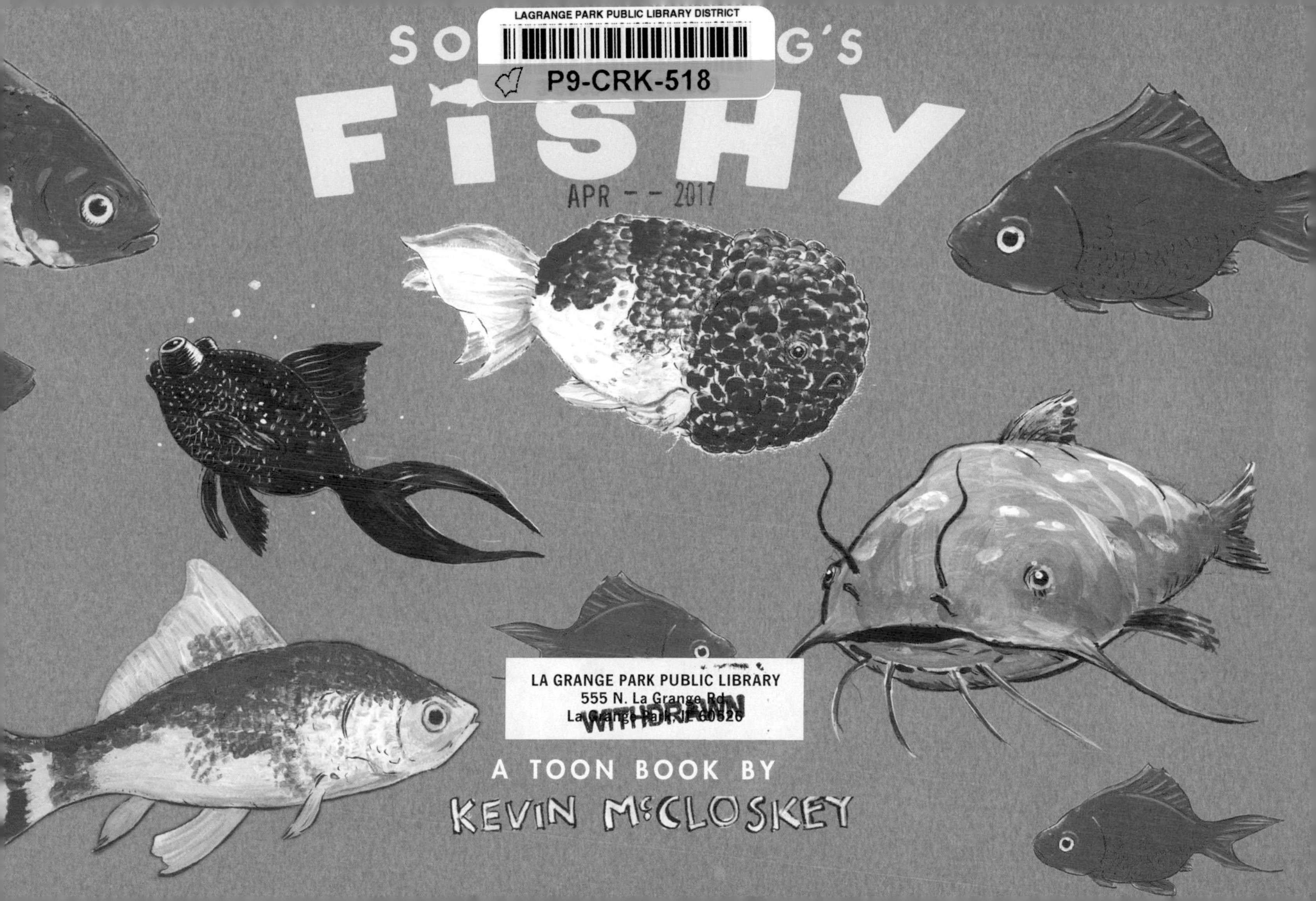
SO G'S
FISHY
A TOON BOOK BY
KEVIN McCLOSKEY

BIG FISH, SMALL FISH—THERE ARE SO MANY KINDS OF FISH. HERE'S ONE FOR EVERY LETTER OF THE ALPHABET.

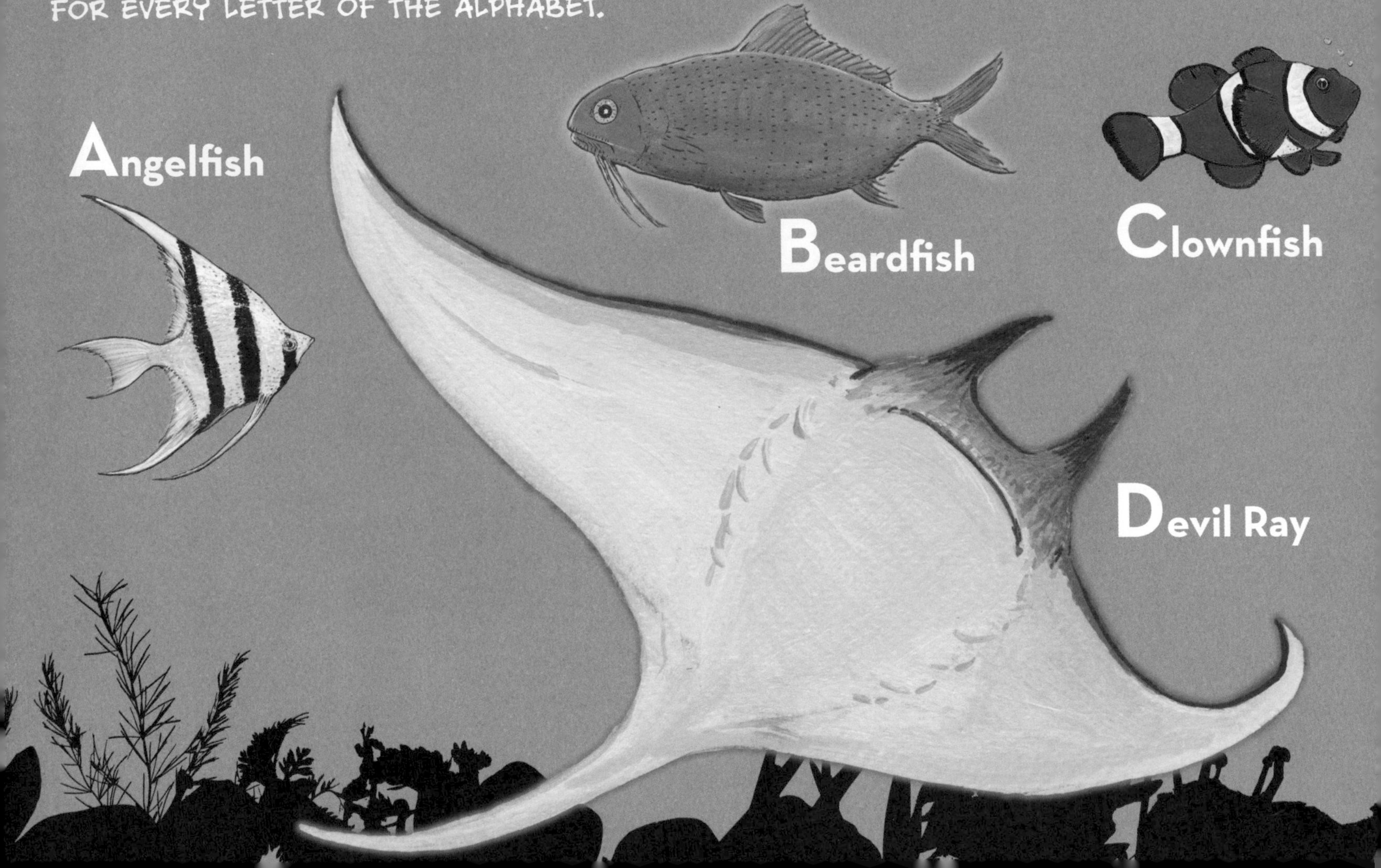
Angelfish
Beardfish
Clownfish
Devil Ray

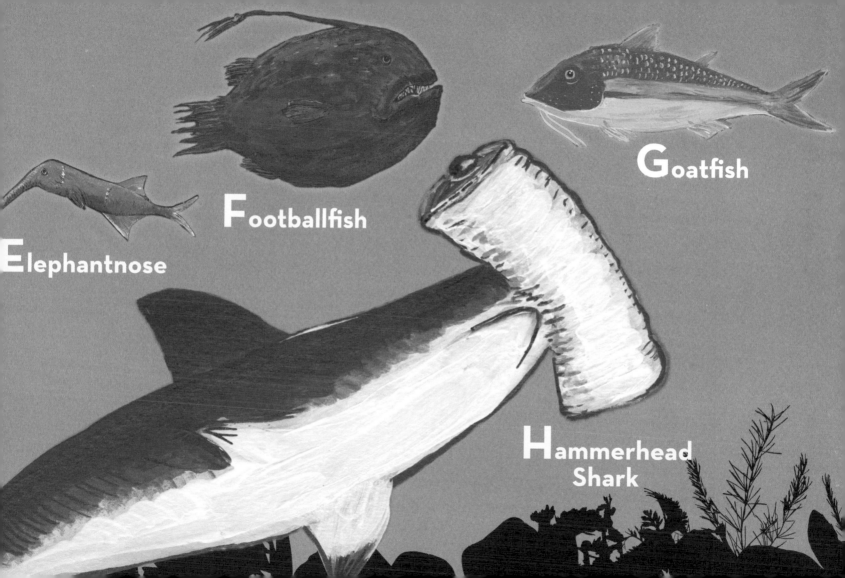

Elephantnose

Footballfish

Goatfish

Hammerhead
Shark

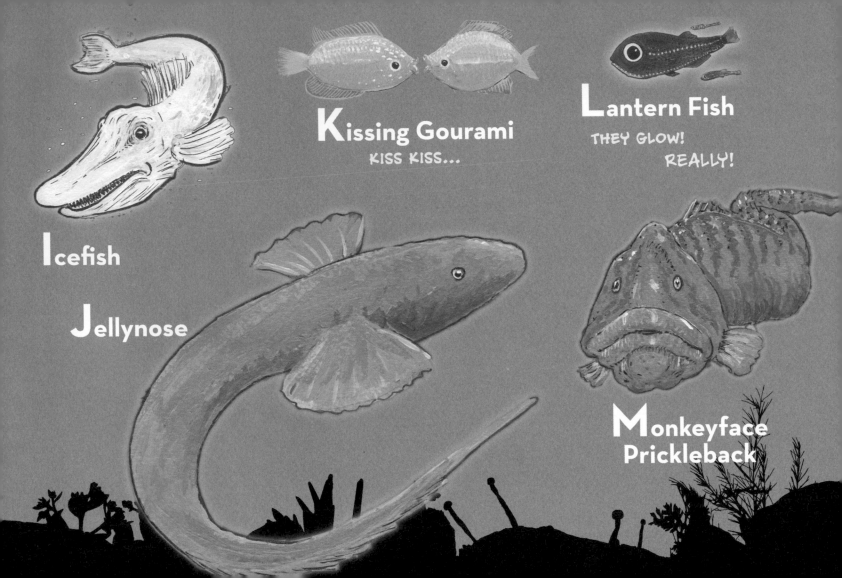

Icefish

Jellynose

Kissing Gourami
KISS KISS...

Lantern Fish
THEY GLOW!
REALLY!

Monkeyface
Prickleback

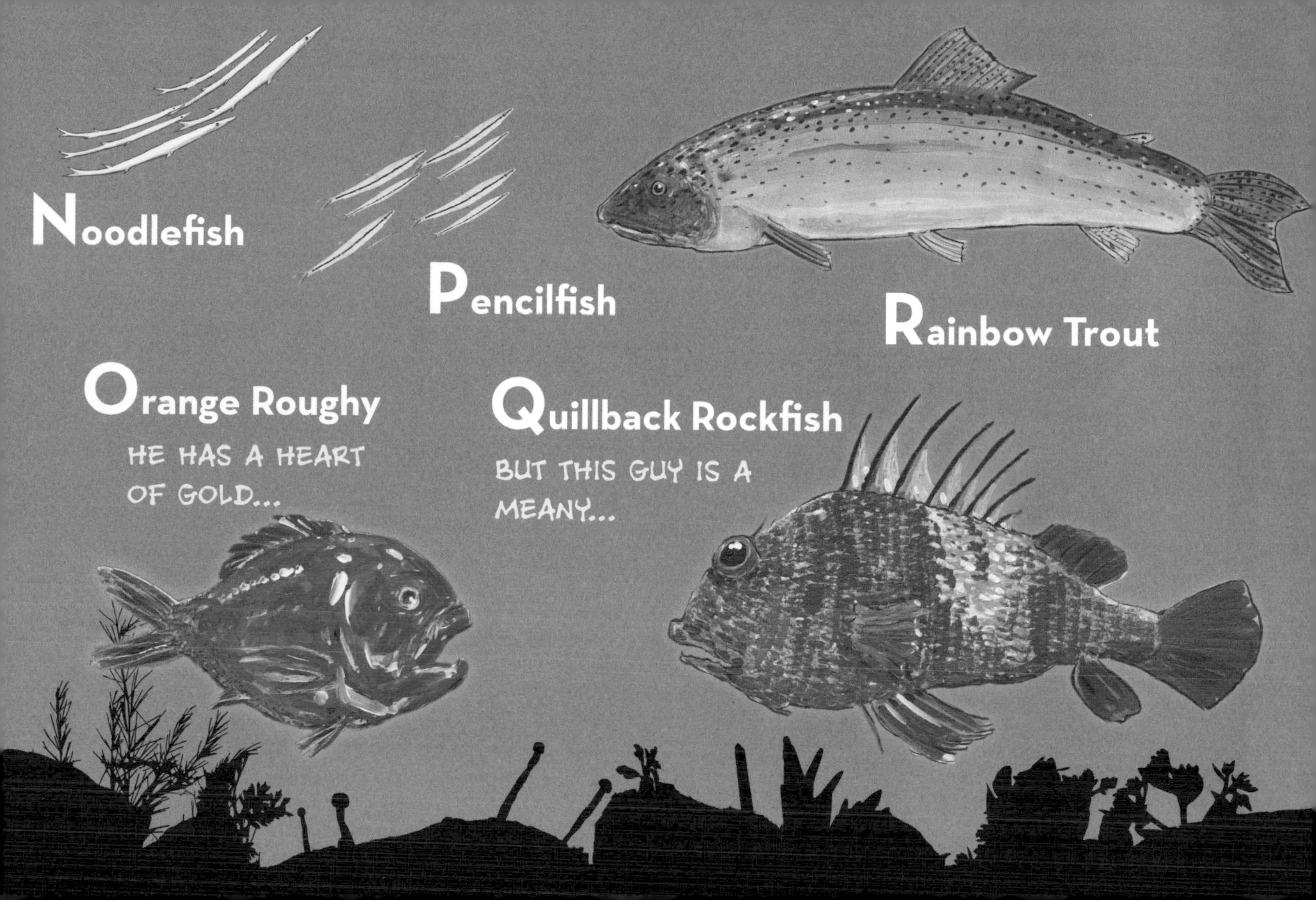
Noodlefish
Pencilfish
Rainbow Trout
Orange Roughy
HE HAS A HEART OF GOLD...
Quillback Rockfish
BUT THIS GUY IS A MEANY...

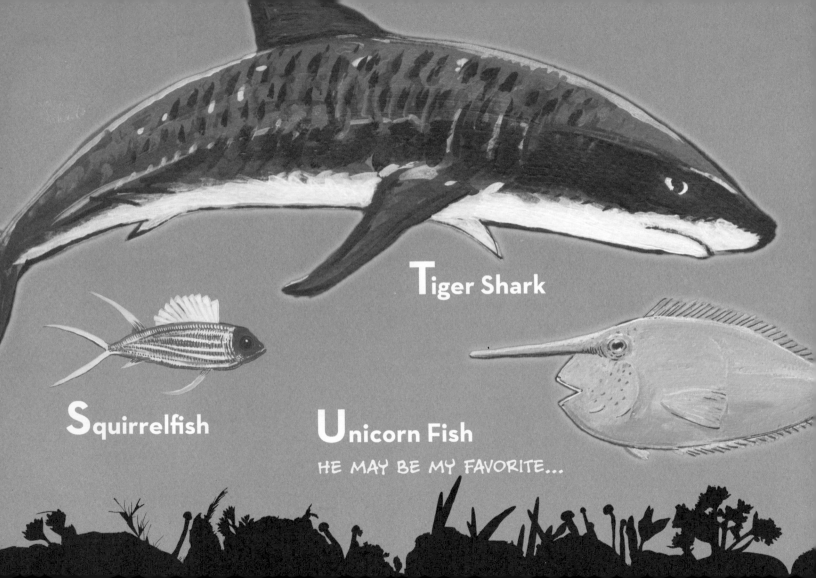

Tiger Shark

Squirrelfish

Unicorn Fish

HE MAY BE MY FAVORITE...

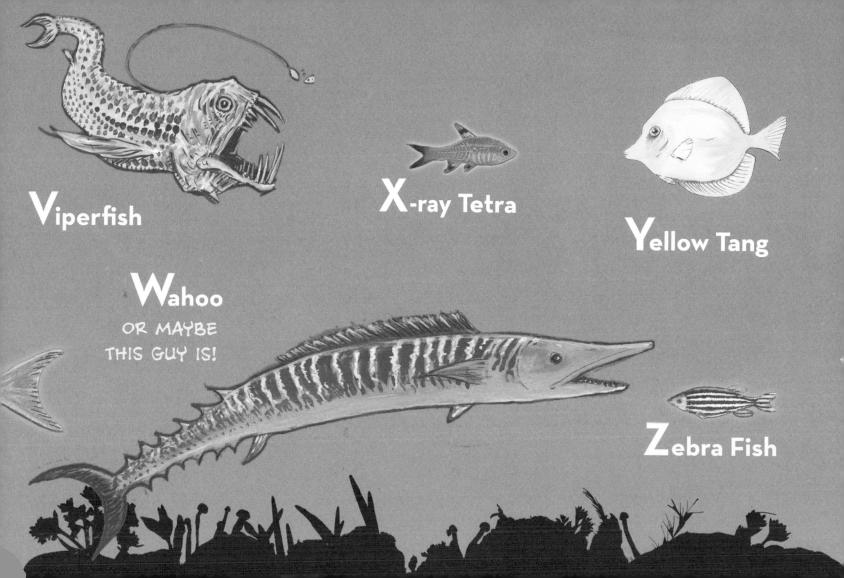

Viperfish

X-ray Tetra

Yellow Tang

Wahoo
OR MAYBE
THIS GUY IS!

Zebra Fish

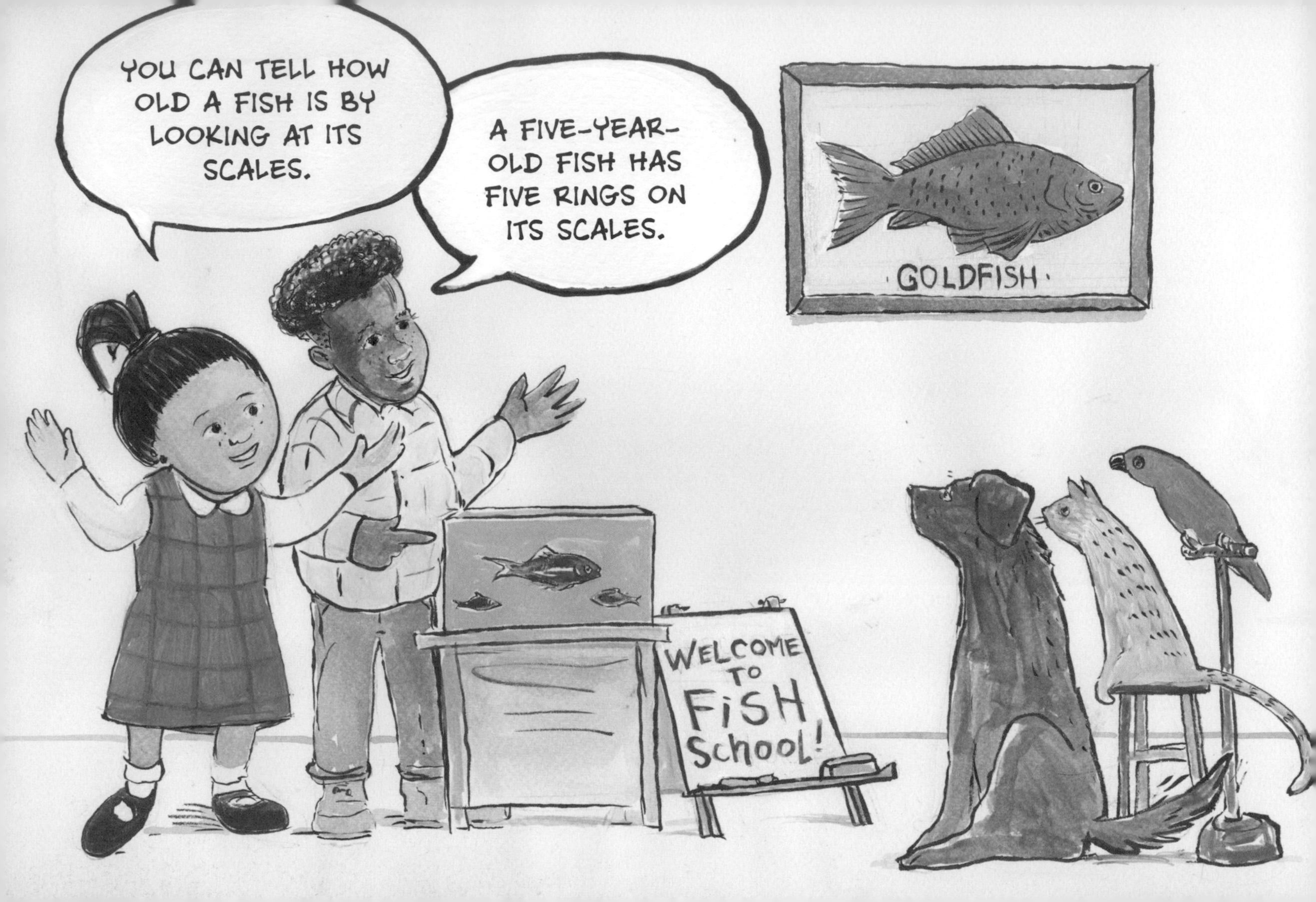
YOU CAN TELL HOW OLD A FISH IS BY LOOKING AT ITS SCALES.
A FIVE-YEAR-OLD FISH HAS FIVE RINGS ON ITS SCALES.
GOLDFISH
WELCOME TO FISH School!

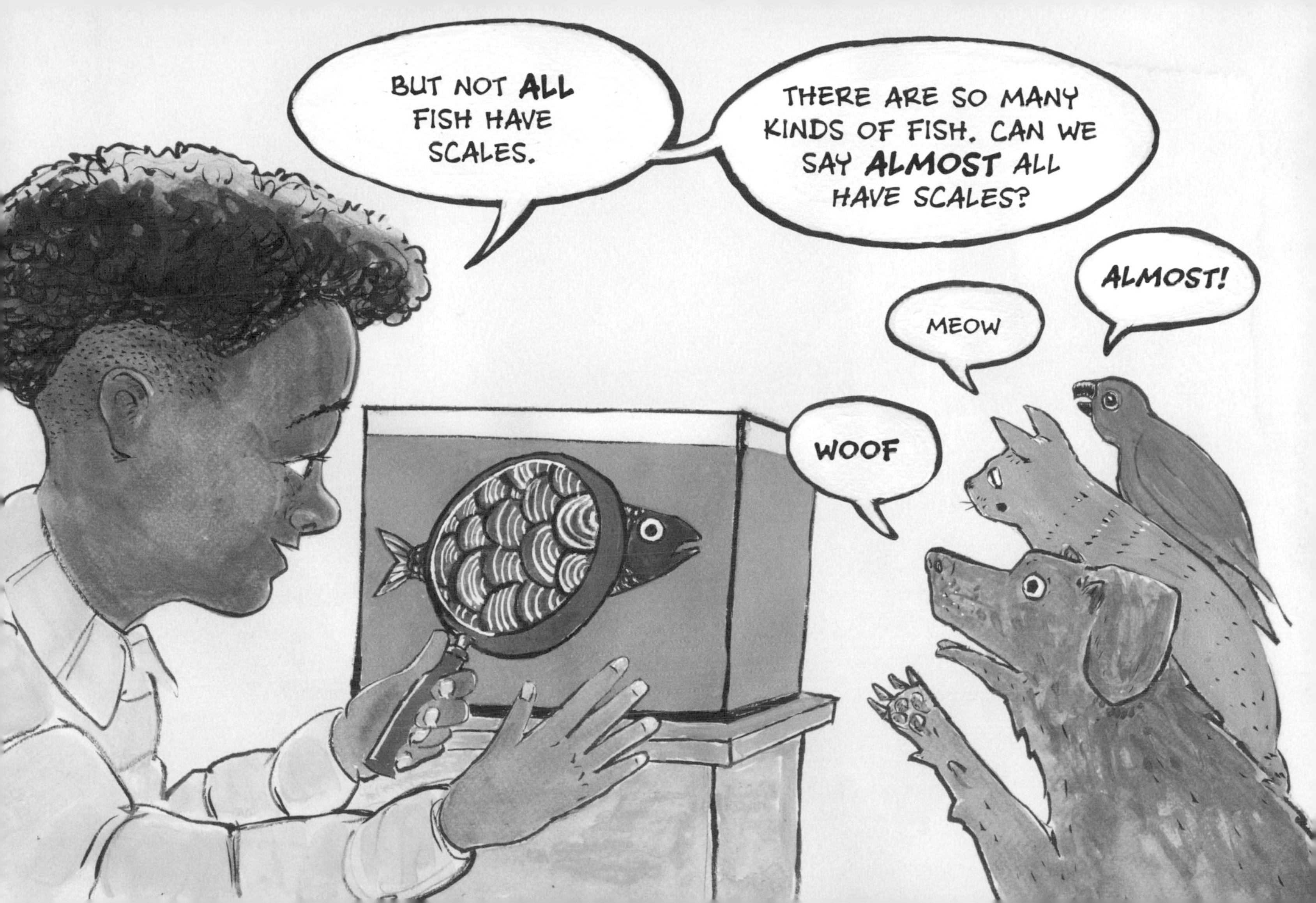
BUT NOT **ALL** FISH HAVE SCALES.
THERE ARE SO MANY KINDS OF FISH. CAN WE SAY **ALMOST** ALL HAVE SCALES?
WOOF
MEOW
ALMOST!

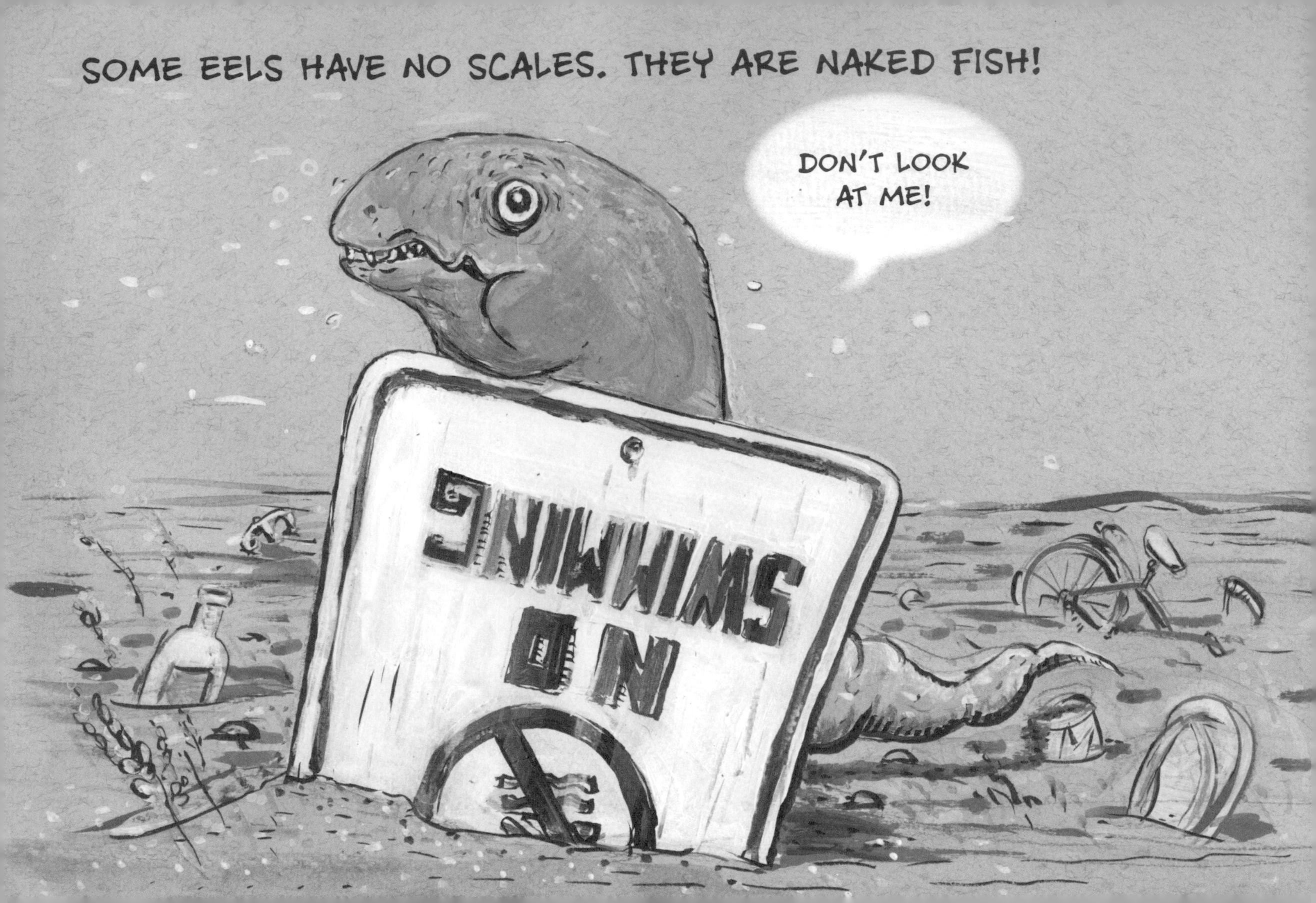
SOME EELS HAVE NO SCALES. THEY ARE NAKED FISH!
DON'T LOOK AT ME!

ALL FISH ARE VERTEBRATES–THAT MEANS THEY HAVE BONES.
ALMOST ALL FISH! THE HAGFISH IS A FISH WITH NO SPINE!

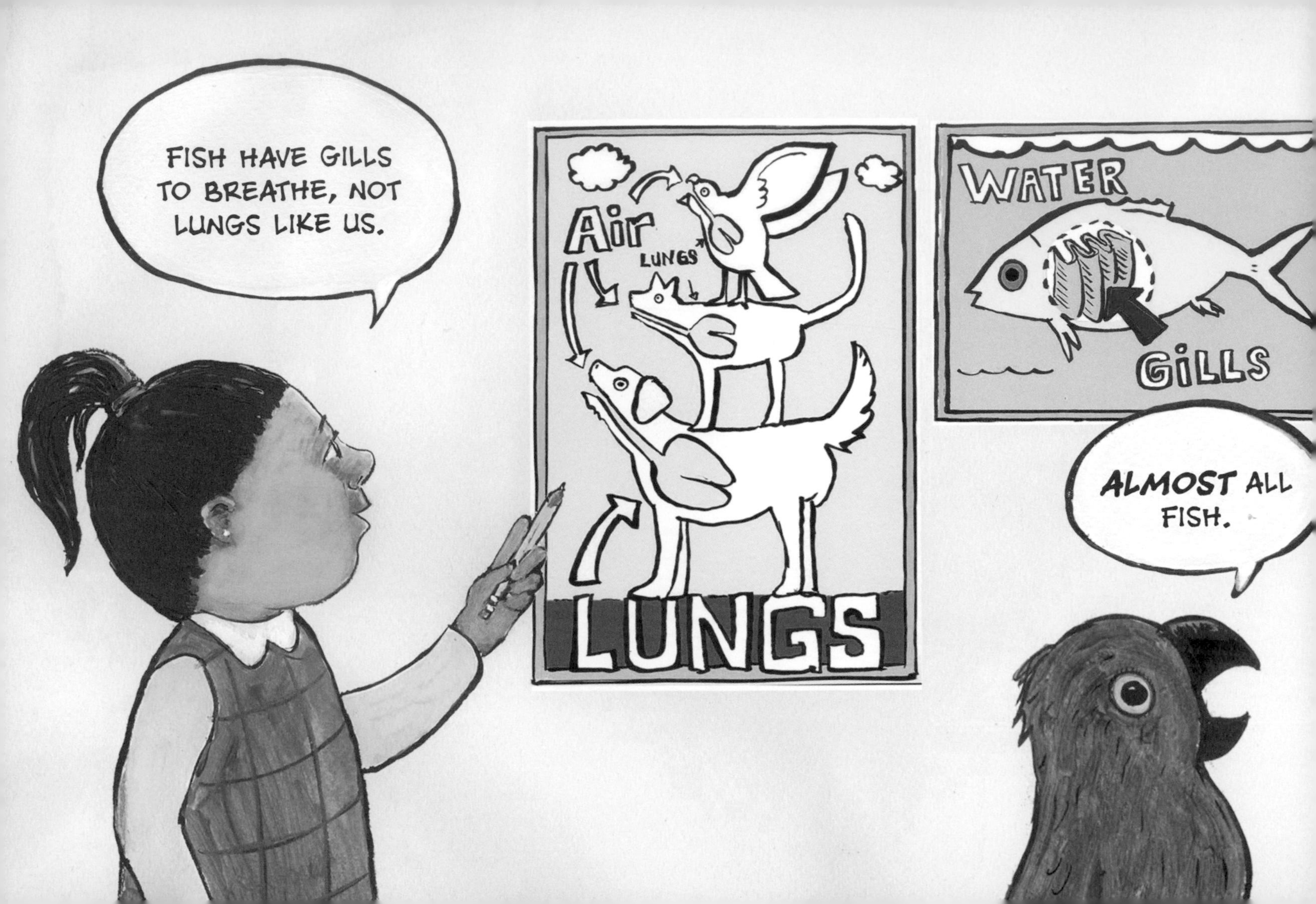
FISH HAVE GILLS TO BREATHE, NOT LUNGS LIKE US.
Air
LUNGS
LUNGS
WATER
GILLS
ALMOST ALL FISH.

LUNGFISH CAN BREATHE WITH THEIR GILLS OR BY GULPING AIR.

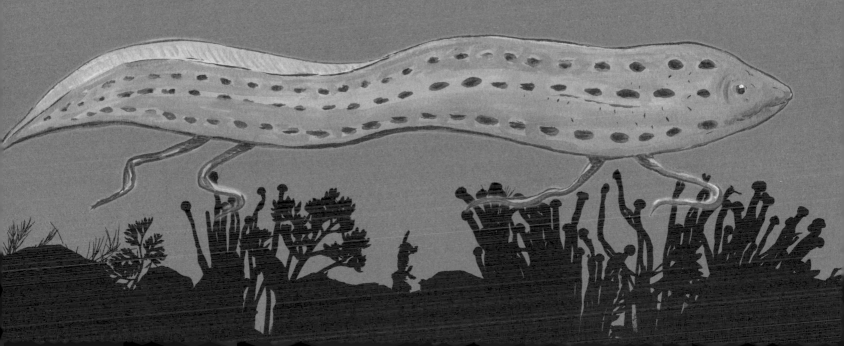

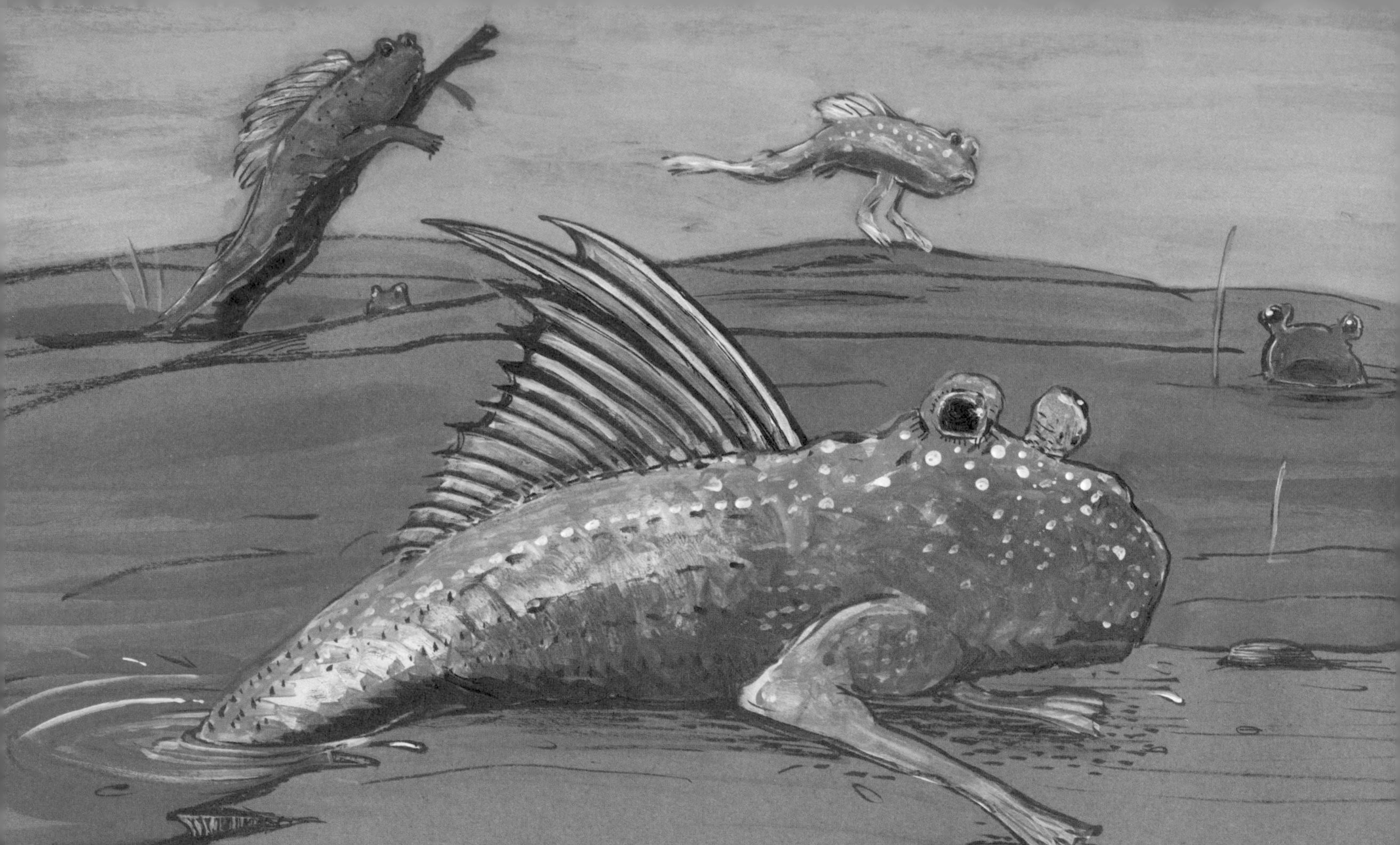

MUDSKIPPERS GO IN AND OUT
OF THE WATER AND WALK ON THEIR FINS.

MOST FISH LIVE ONLY IN WATER,
BUT SOME FISH CAN FLY...

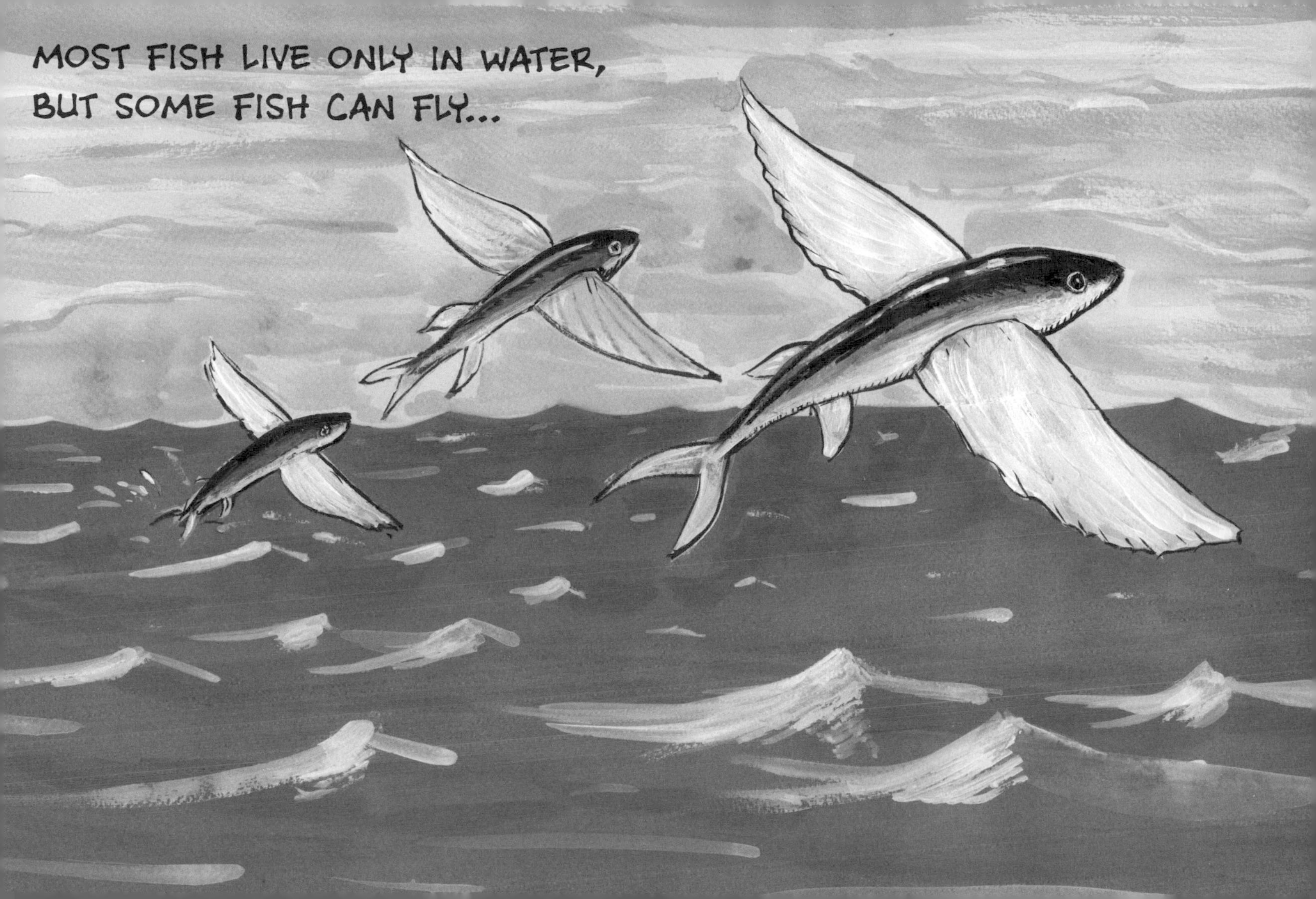

BUT NOT ALL THINGS THAT LIVE IN WATER ARE FISH-LIKE JELLYFISH...

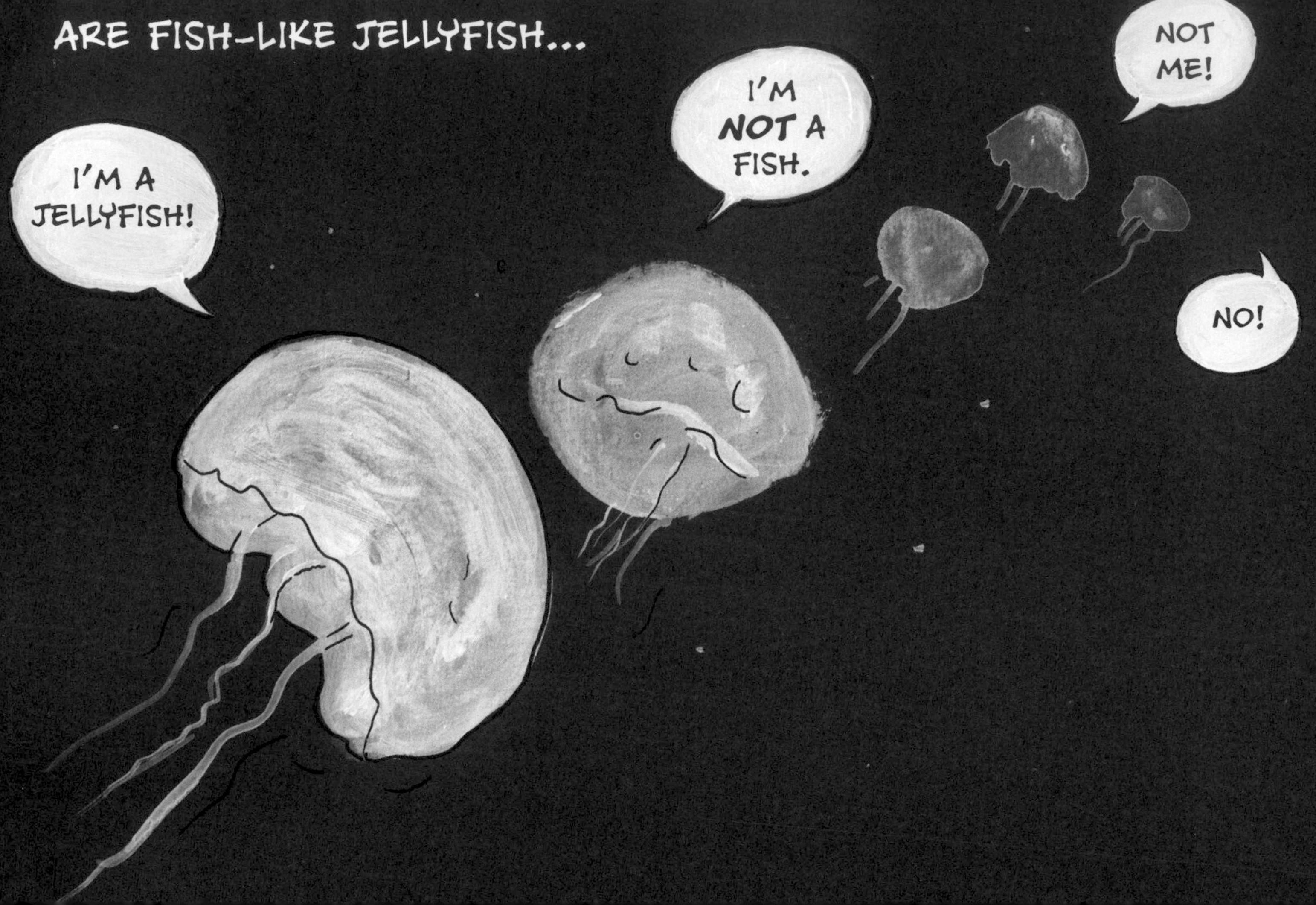
I'M A JELLYFISH!
I'M NOT A FISH.
NOT ME!
NO!

...AND THE CHOCOLATE STARFISH.

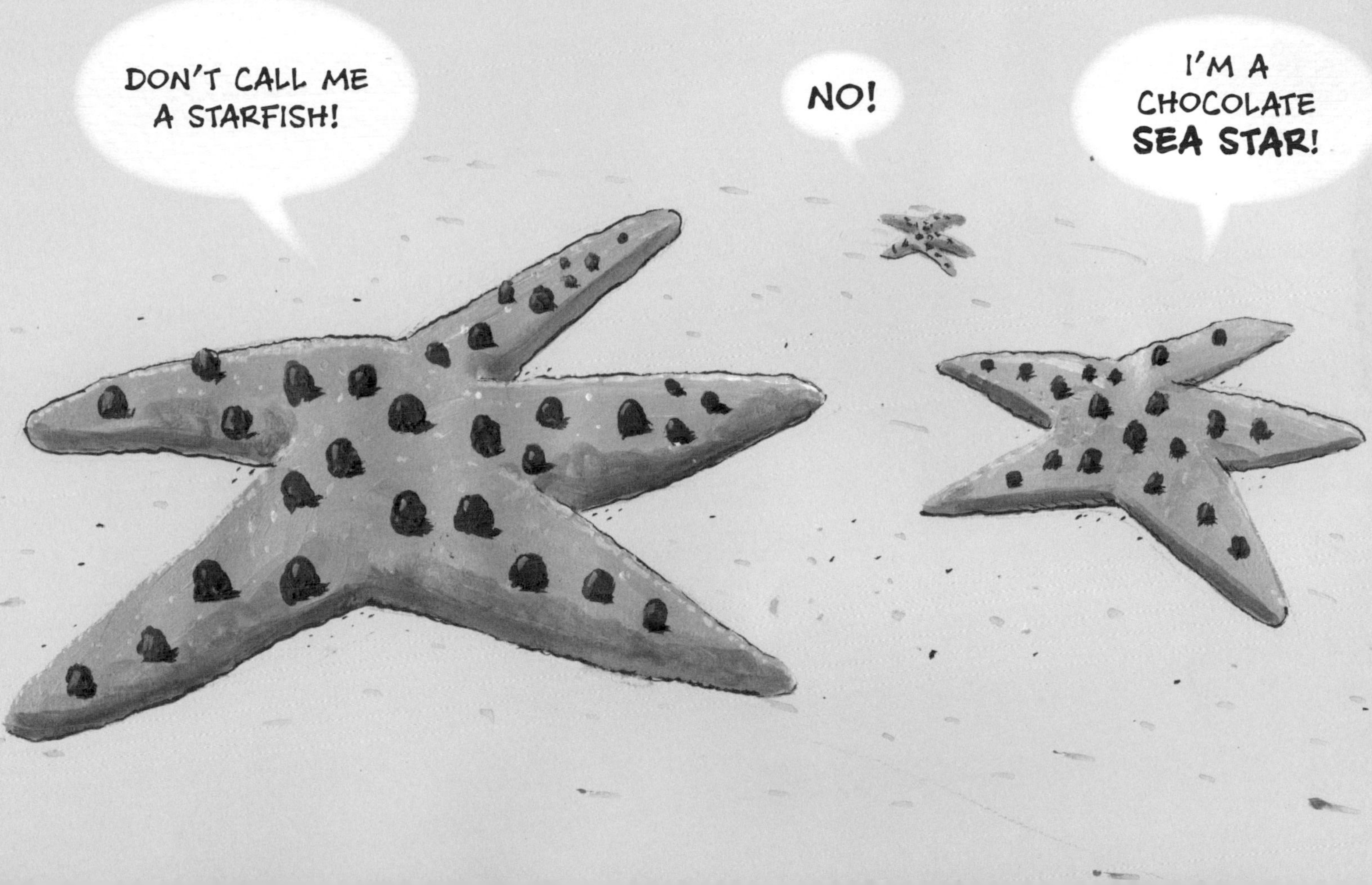
DON'T CALL ME A STARFISH!
NO!
I'M A CHOCOLATE **SEA STAR!**

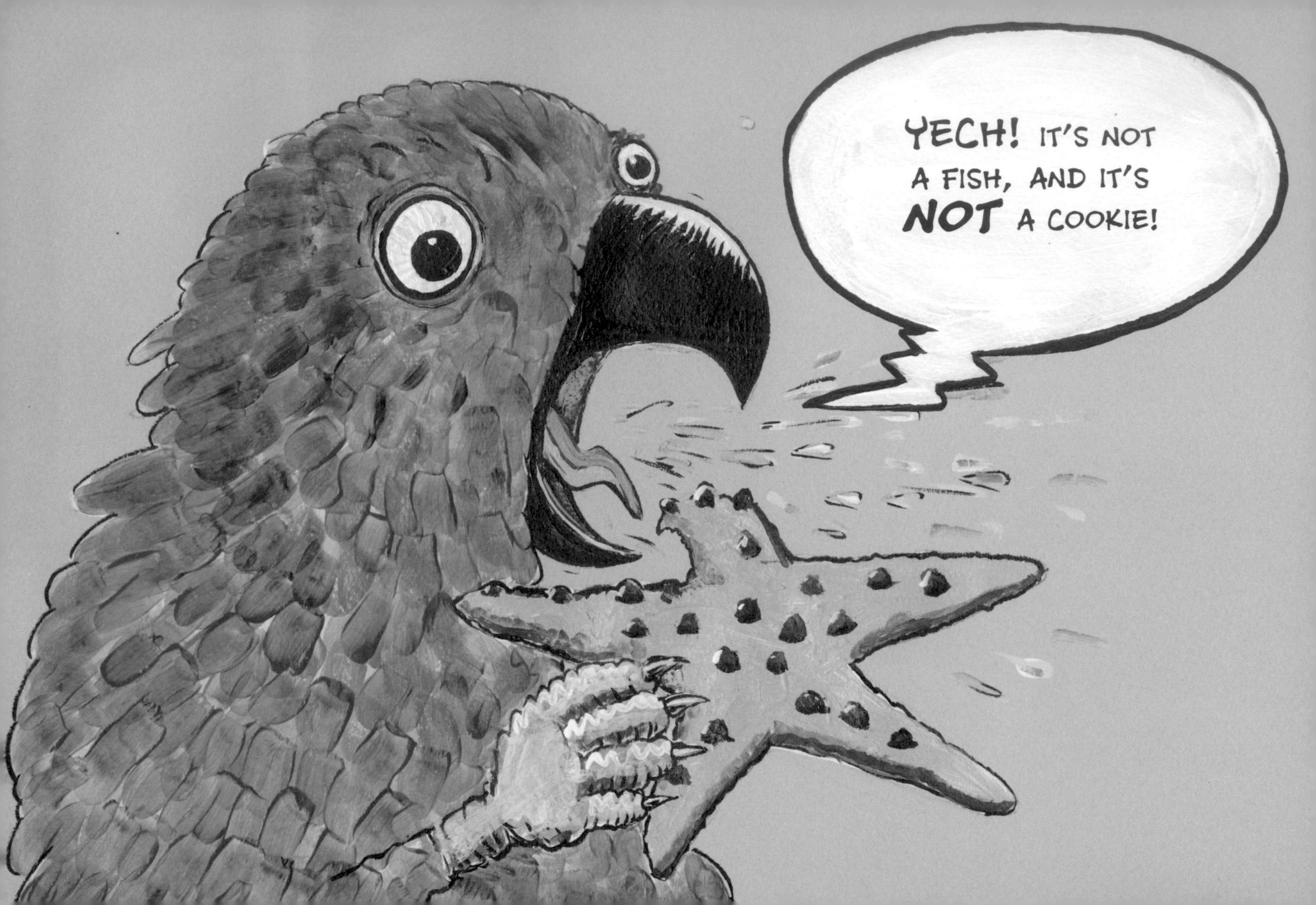
YECH! IT'S NOT A FISH, AND IT'S NOT A COOKIE!

SOME FISH DON'T LOOK LIKE FISH.

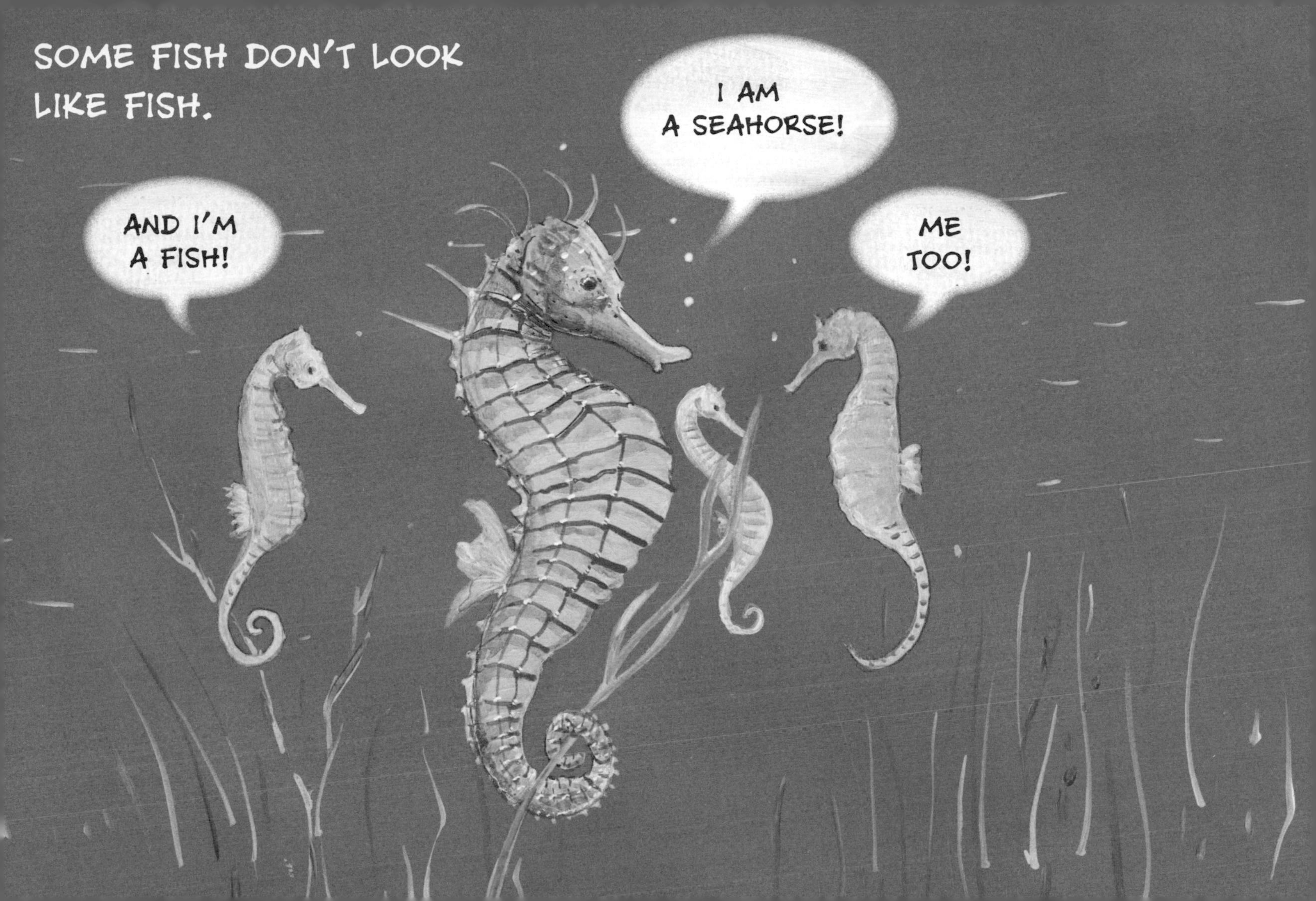
I AM A SEAHORSE!
AND I'M A FISH!
ME TOO!

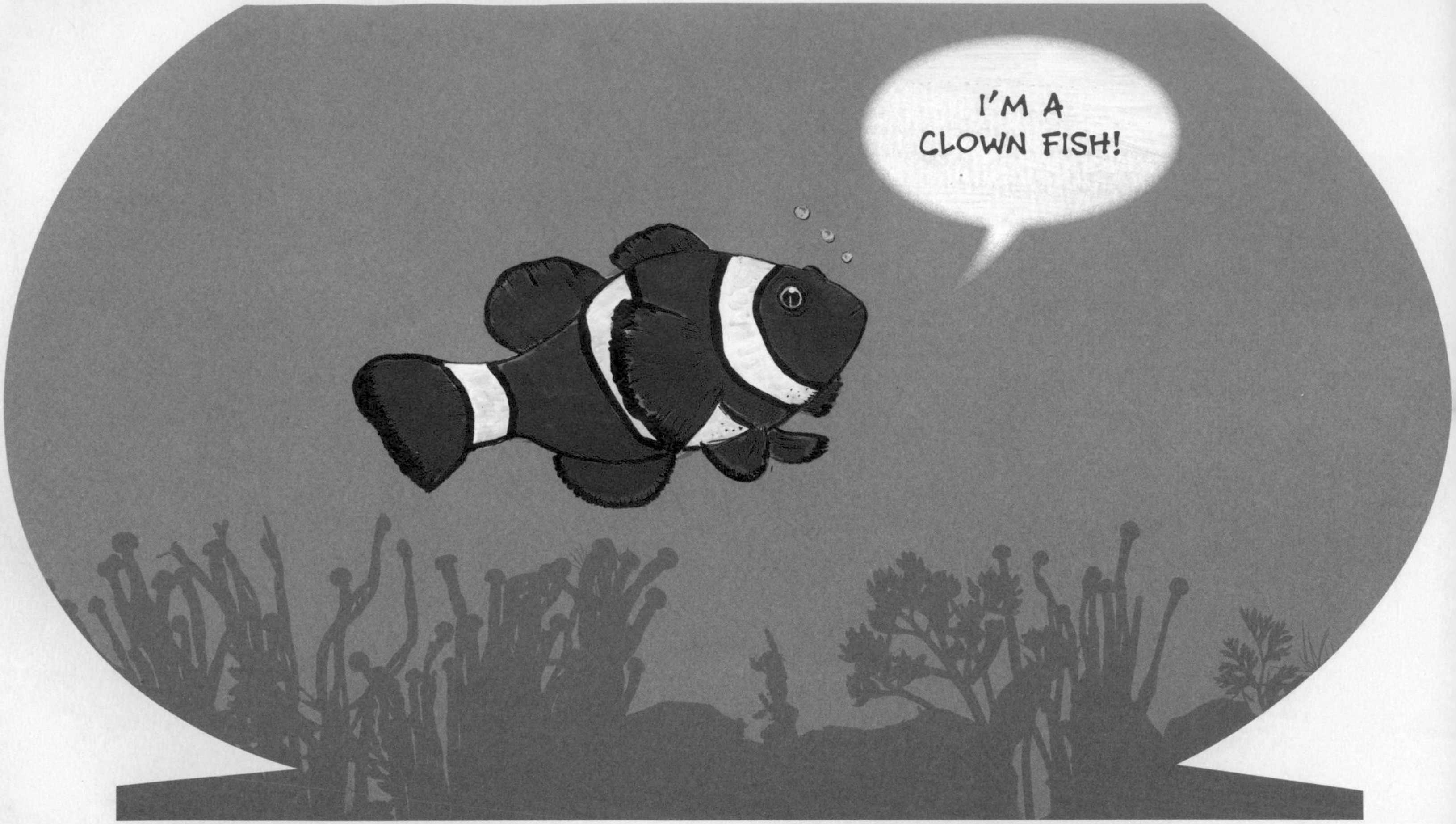
I'M A
CLOWN FISH!

MANY PEOPLE WANT THE FISH THEY SEE IN CARTOON MOVIES.

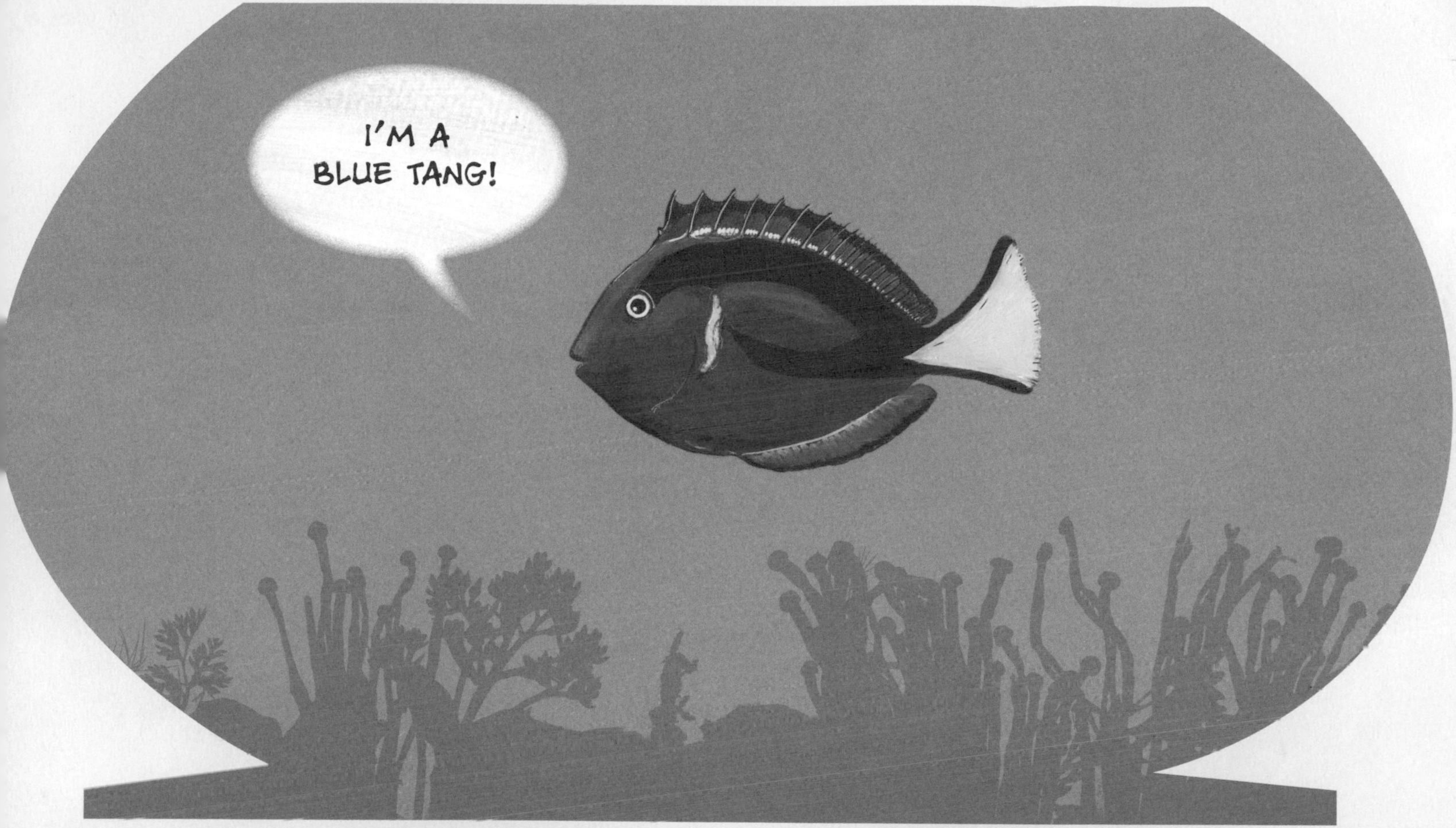
I'M A
BLUE TANG!

THESE ARE RARE AND HARD TO KEEP ALIVE IN A HOME TANK.

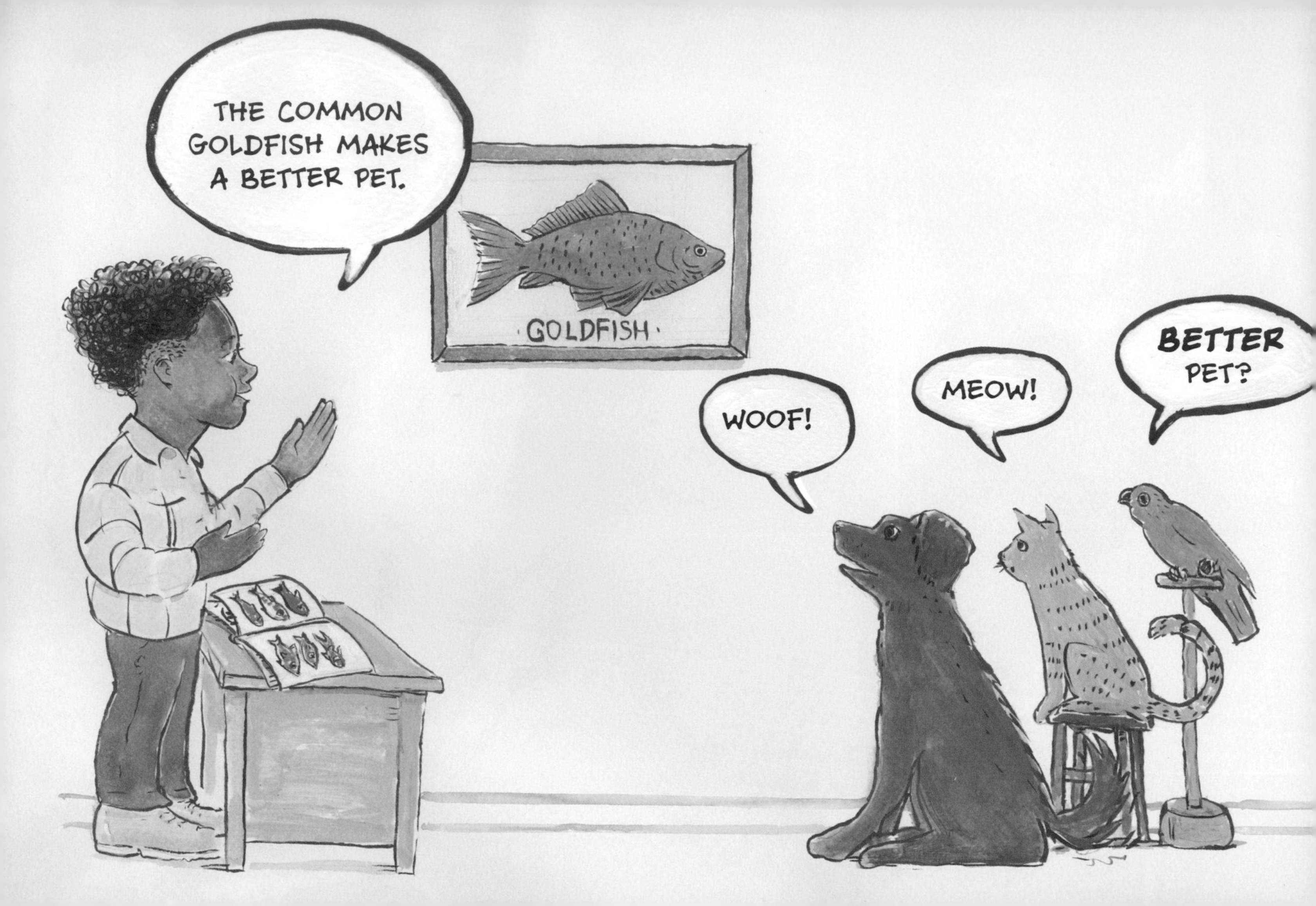
THE COMMON GOLDFISH MAKES A BETTER PET.
GOLDFISH
WOOF!
MEOW!
BETTER PET?

GOLDFISH GET THEIR COLOR FROM THE SUN.

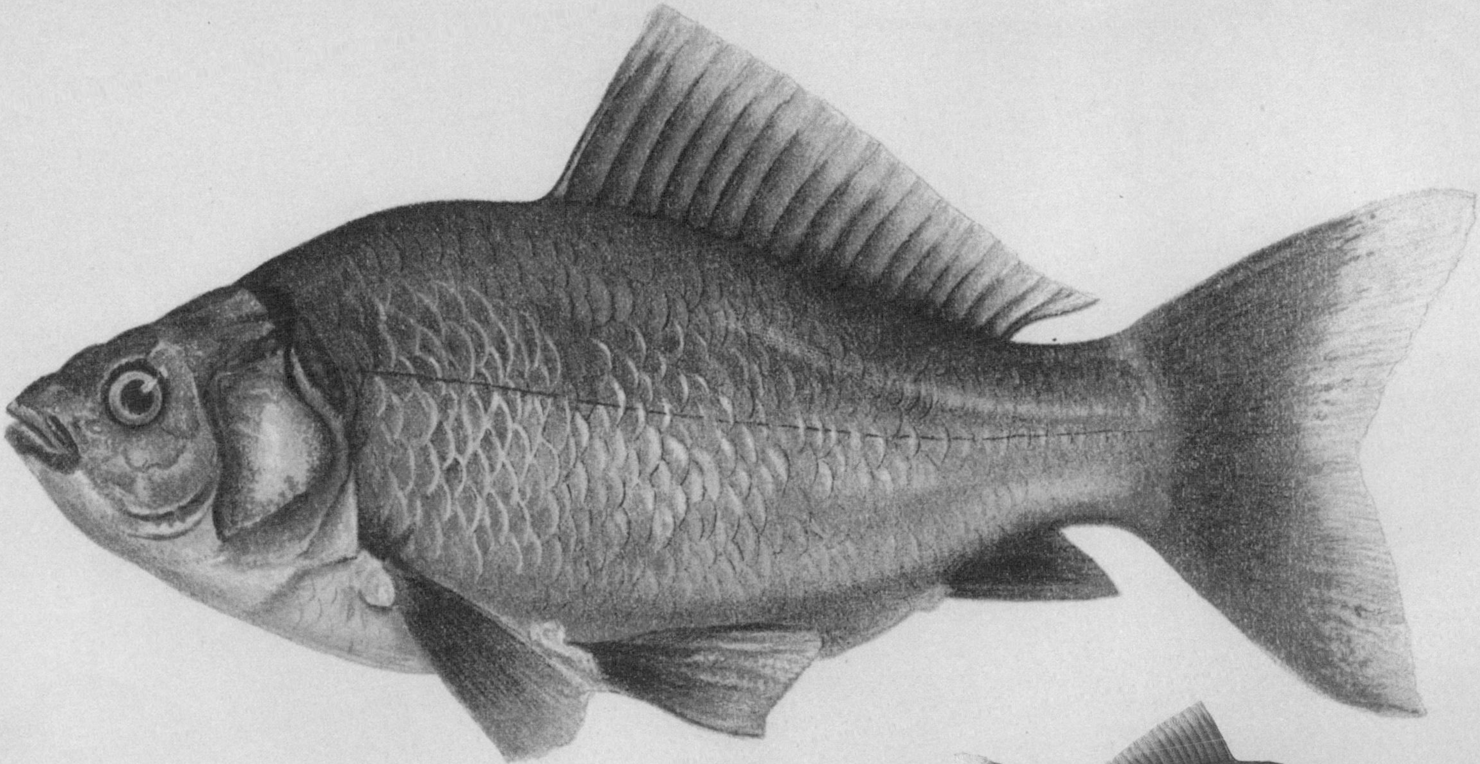

WITHOUT THE SUN, THEY'D BE **BLACK** FISH.

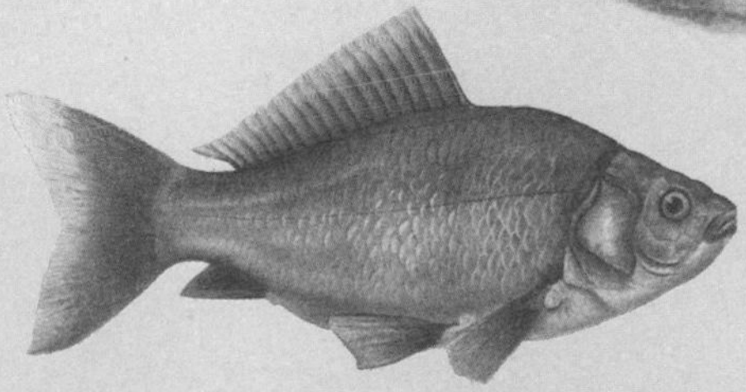

LONG AGO, A FEW SHINY **GOLD** FISHES WERE FOUND IN CHINA.

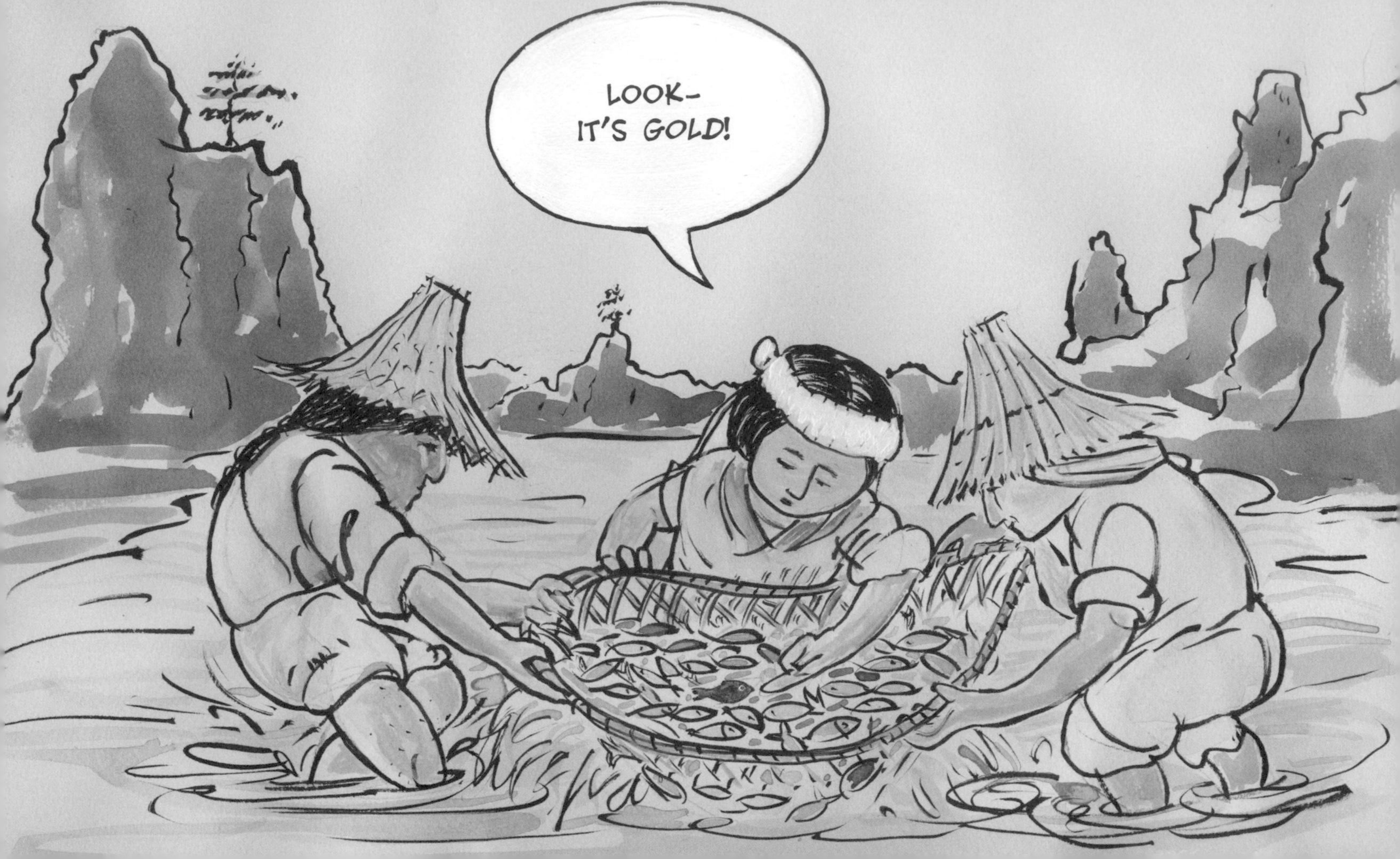
LOOK-
IT'S GOLD!

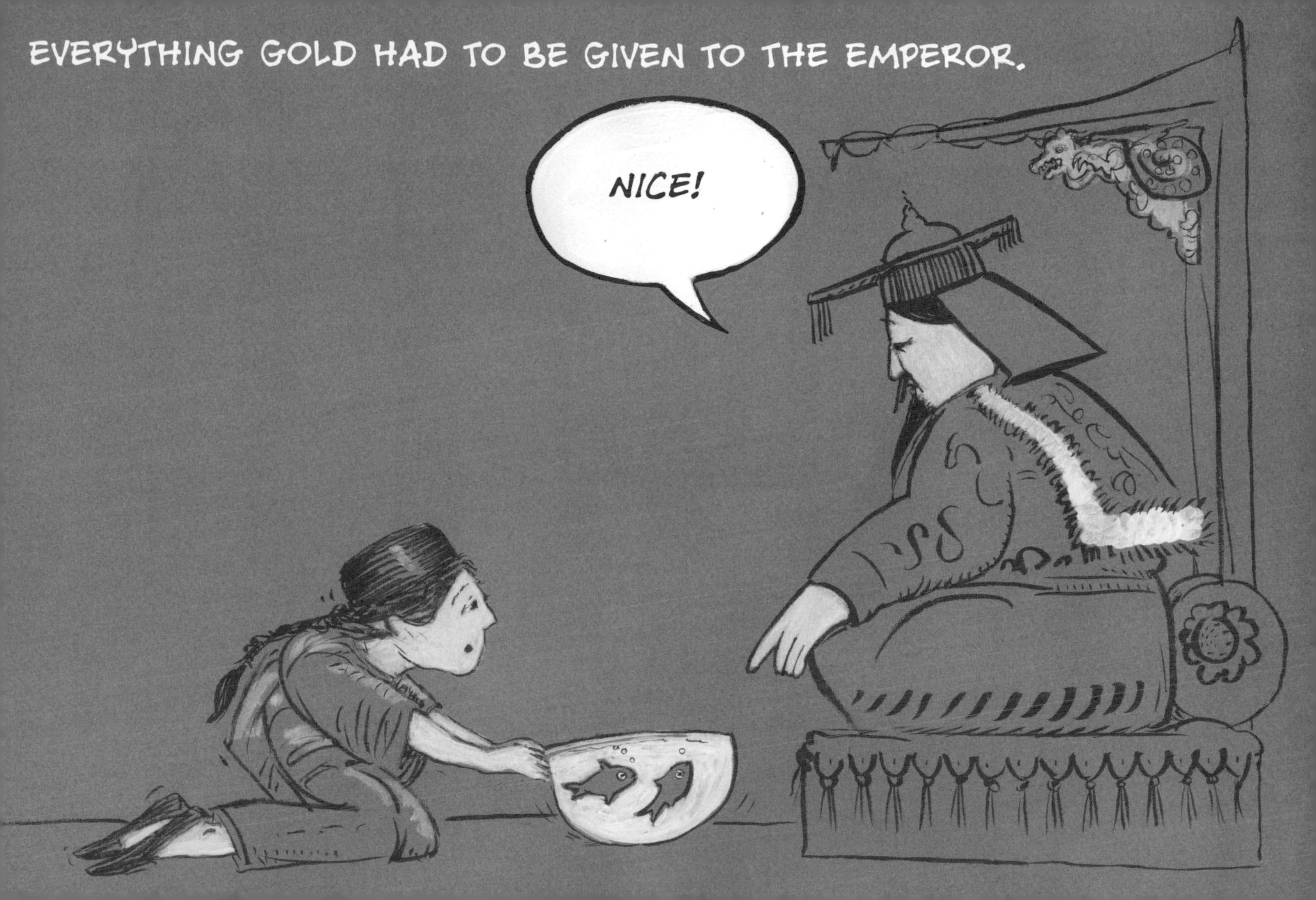
EVERYTHING GOLD HAD TO BE GIVEN TO THE EMPEROR.
NICE!

WHEN GOLDFISH CAME TO EUROPE, THERE WERE VERY FEW. THEY WERE GIVEN AS **VERY** SPECIAL GIFTS.

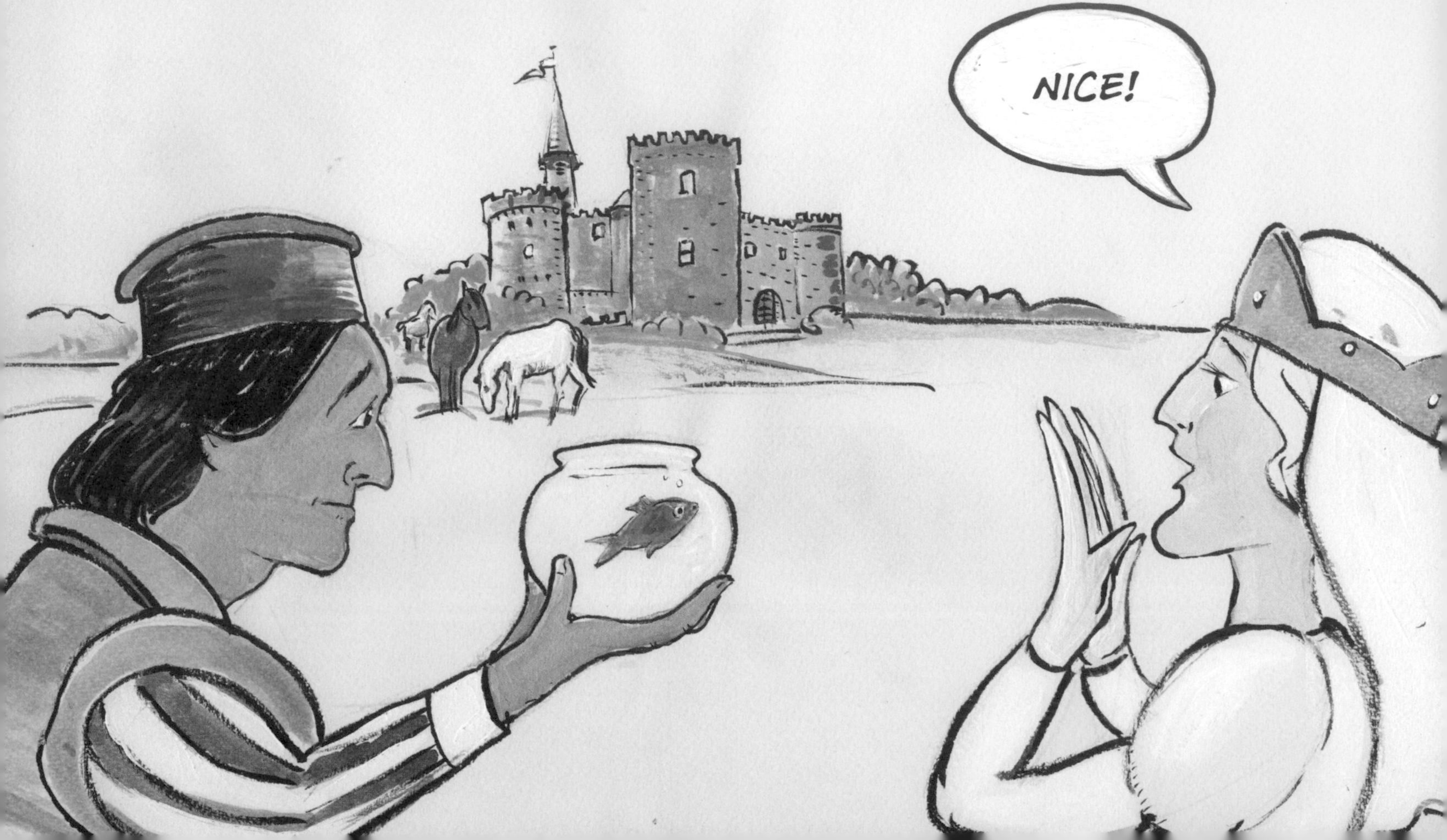
NICE!

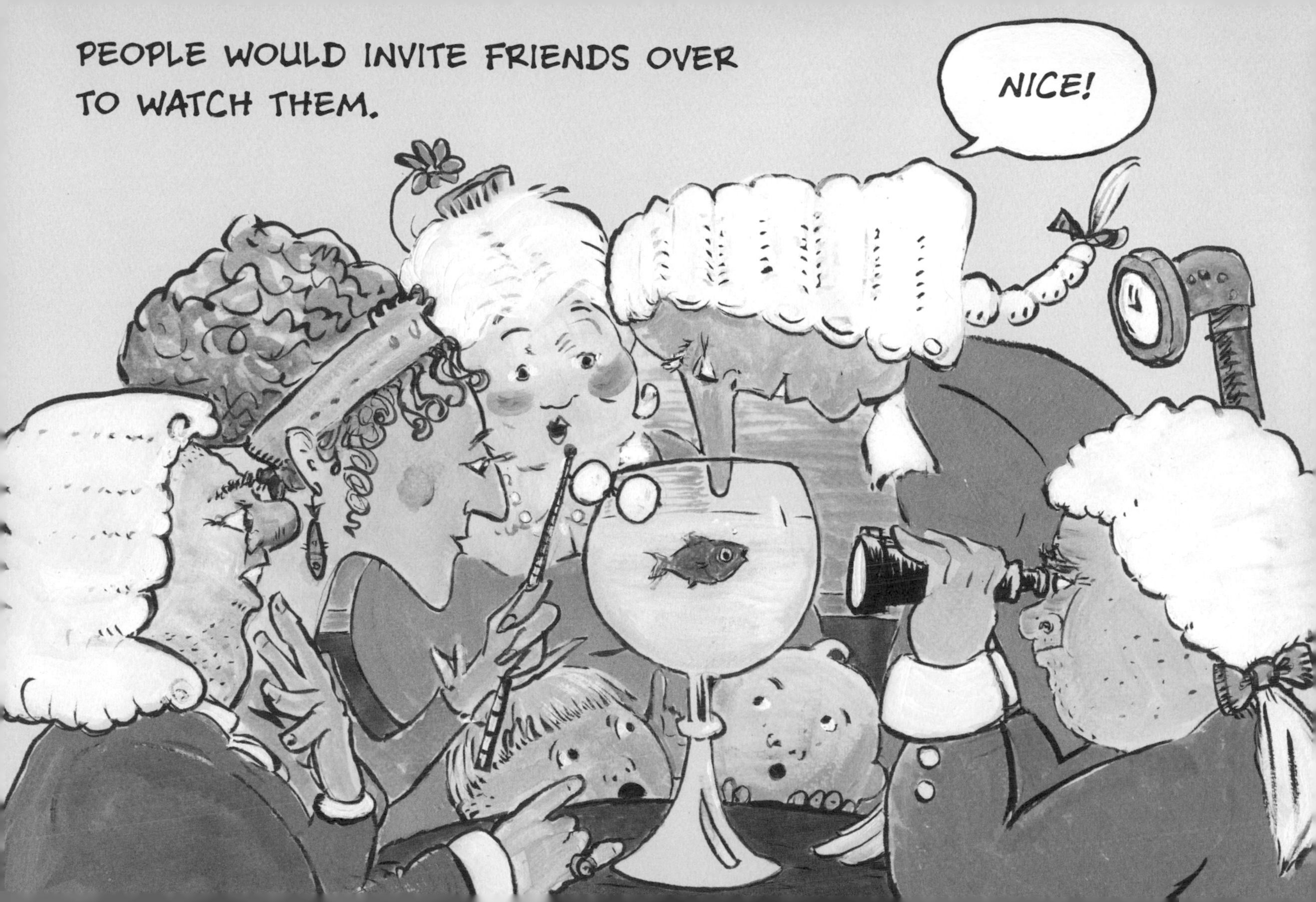
PEOPLE WOULD INVITE FRIENDS OVER TO WATCH THEM.
NICE!

GOLDFISH CAN REMEMBER FACES.

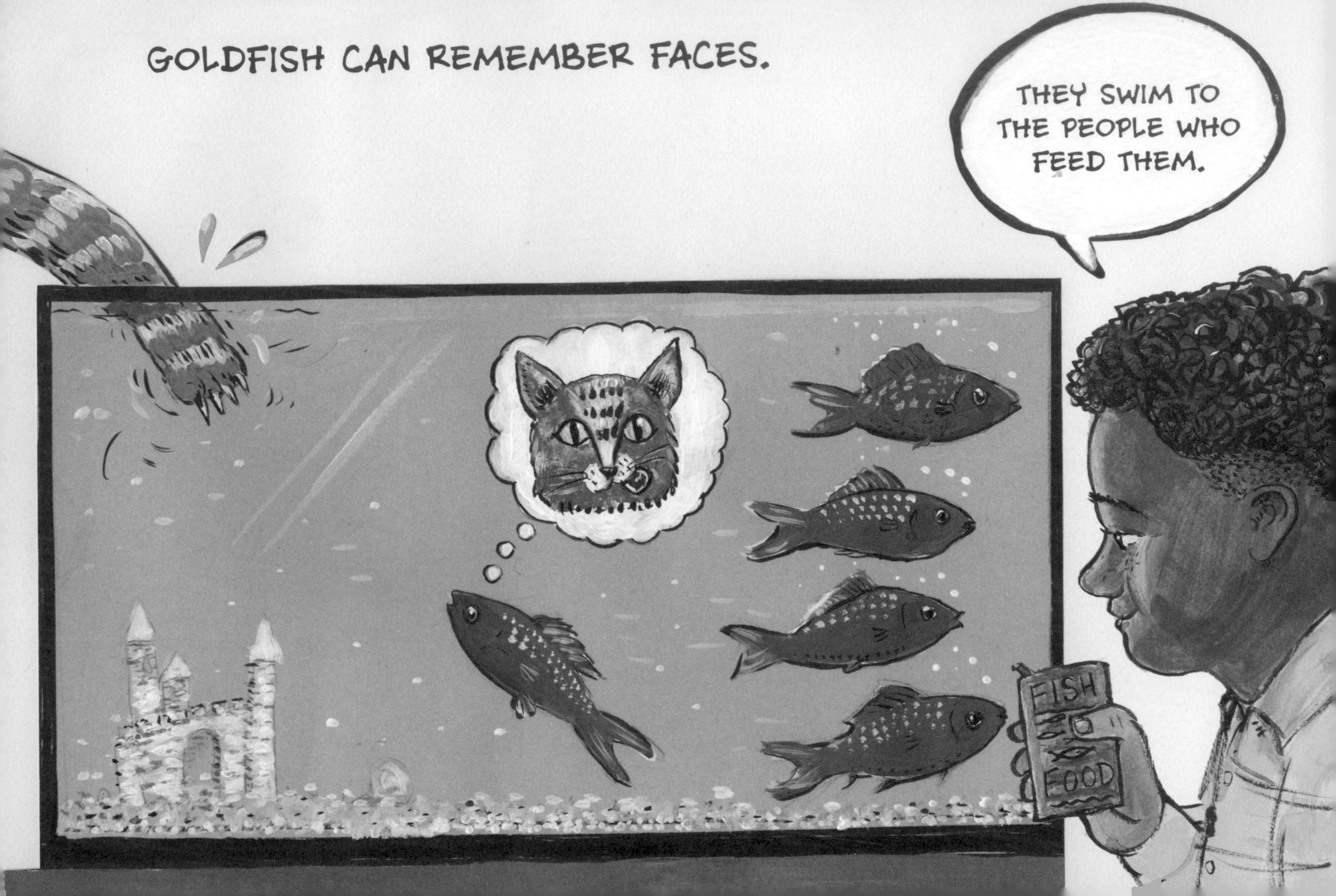
THEY SWIM TO THE PEOPLE WHO FEED THEM.
FISH FOOD

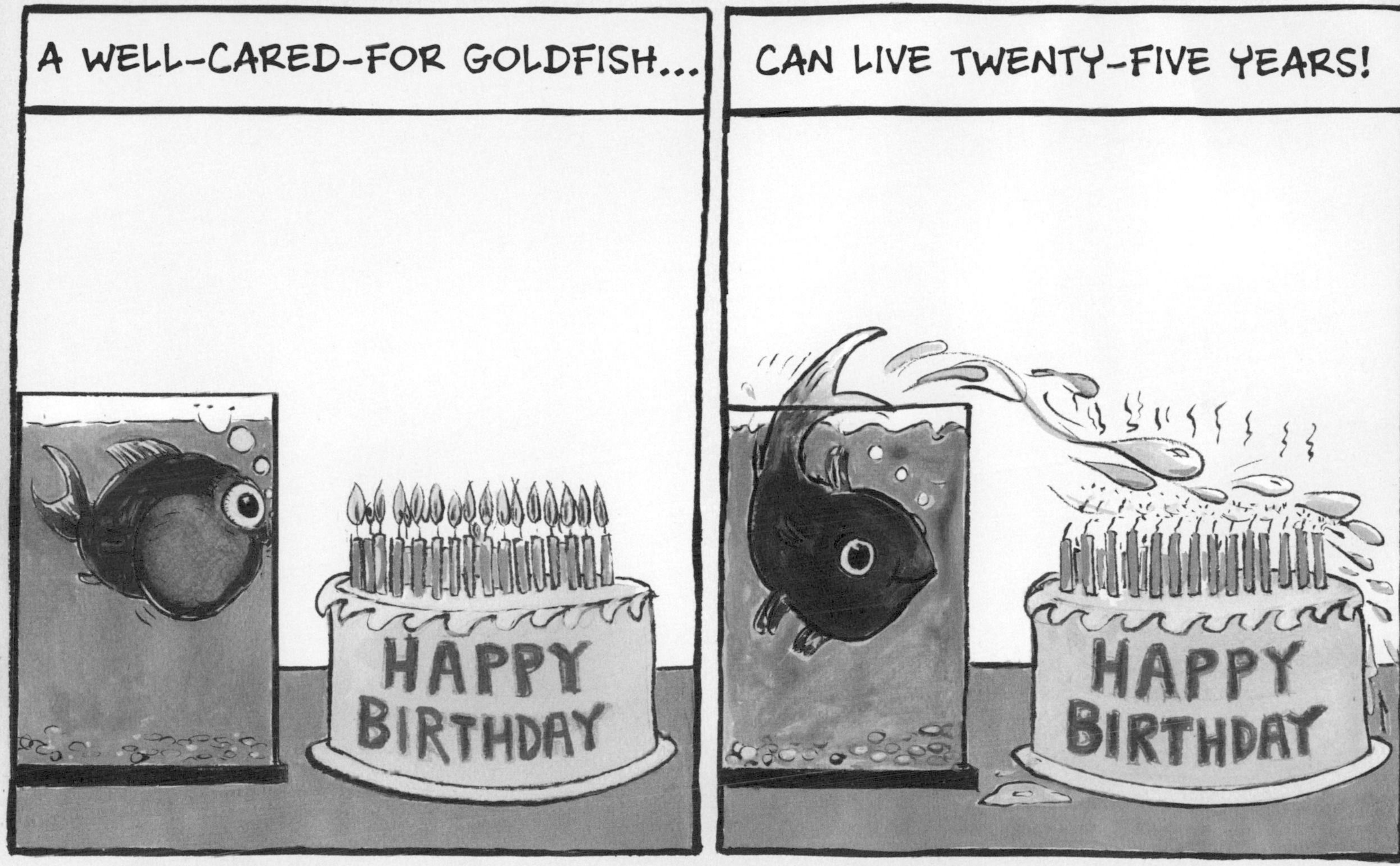
A WELL-CARED-FOR GOLDFISH...
HAPPY BIRTHDAY
CAN LIVE TWENTY-FIVE YEARS!
HAPPY BIRTHDAY

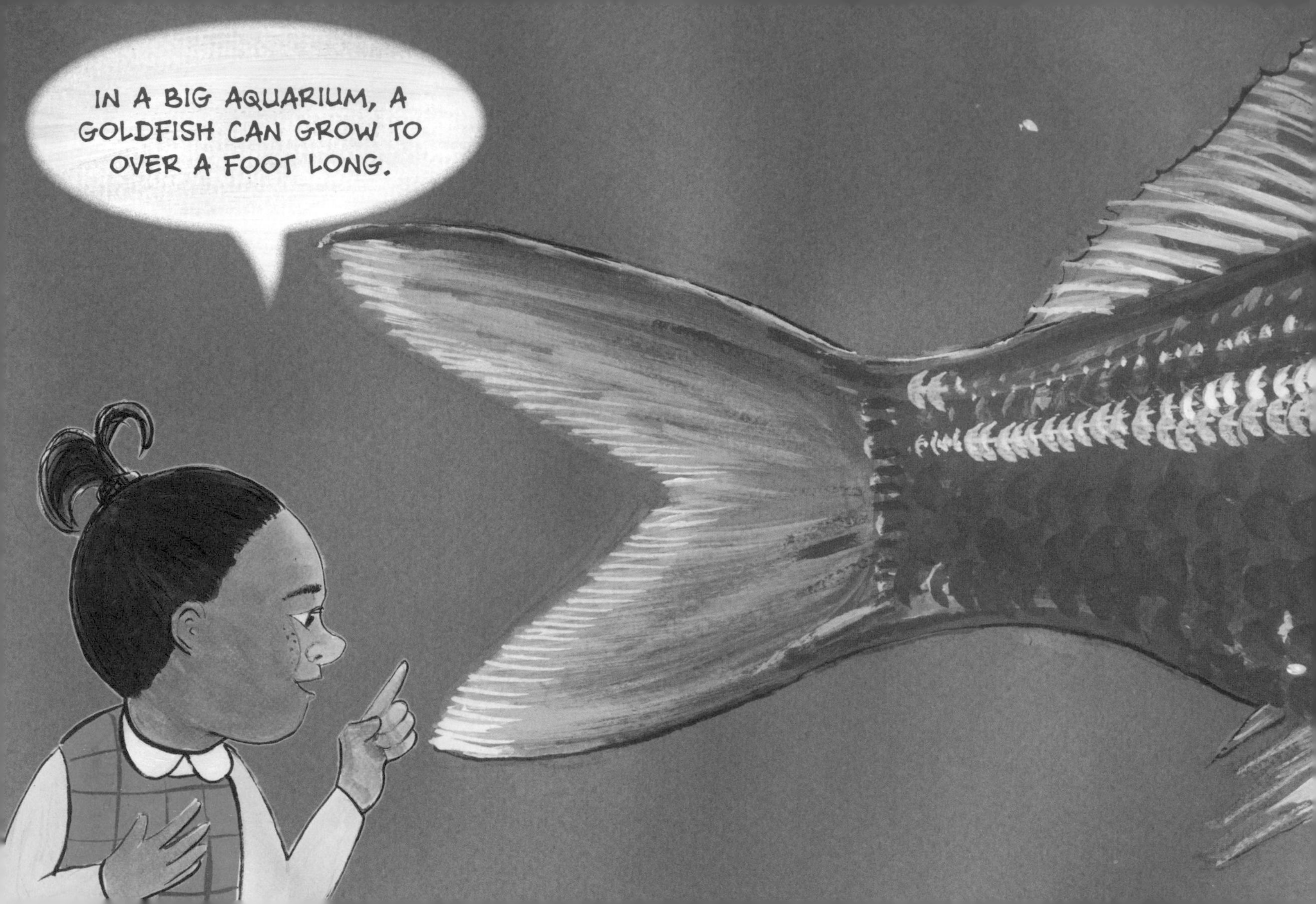
IN A BIG AQUARIUM, A GOLDFISH CAN GROW TO OVER A FOOT LONG.

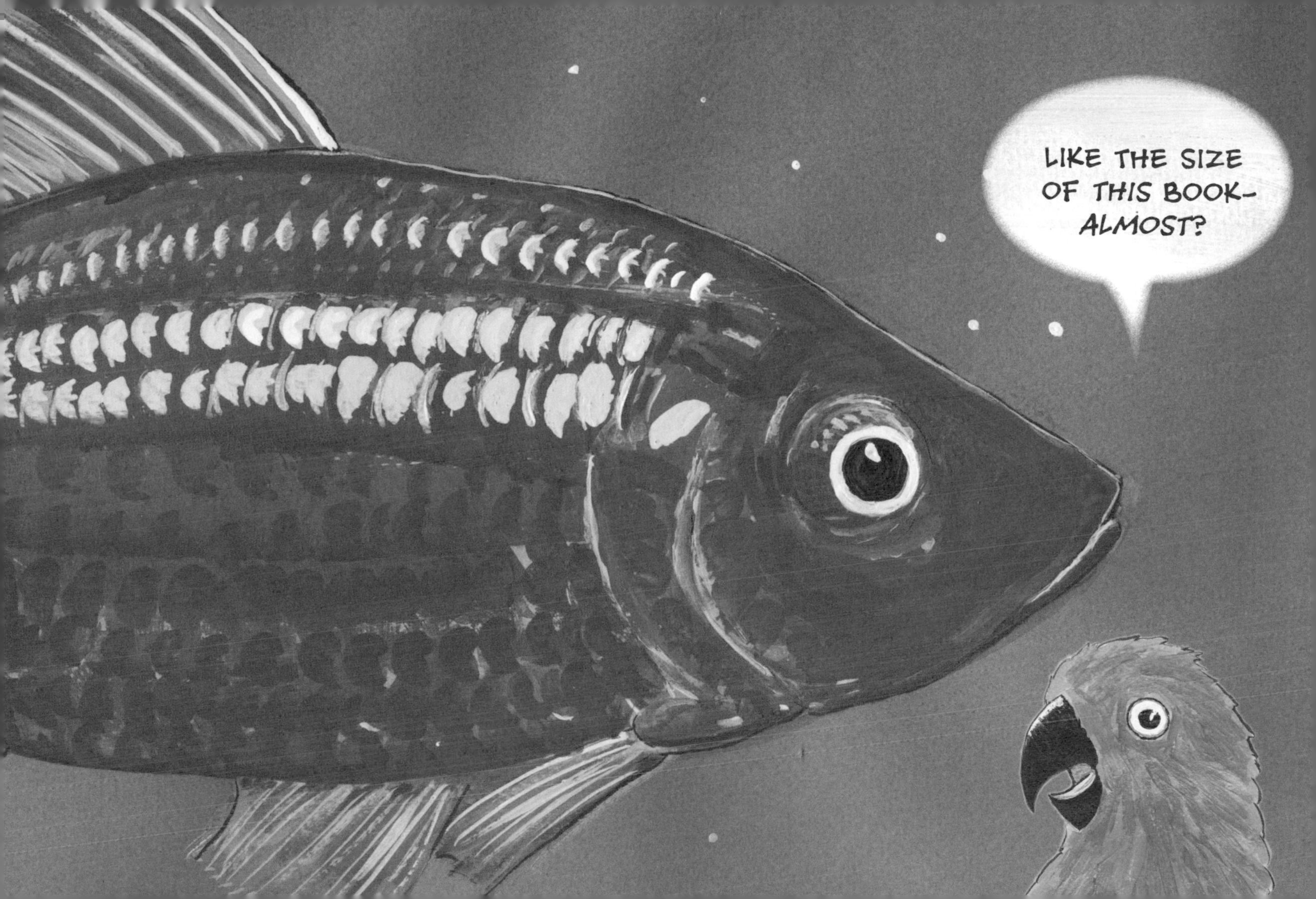
LIKE THE SIZE
OF THIS BOOK-
ALMOST?

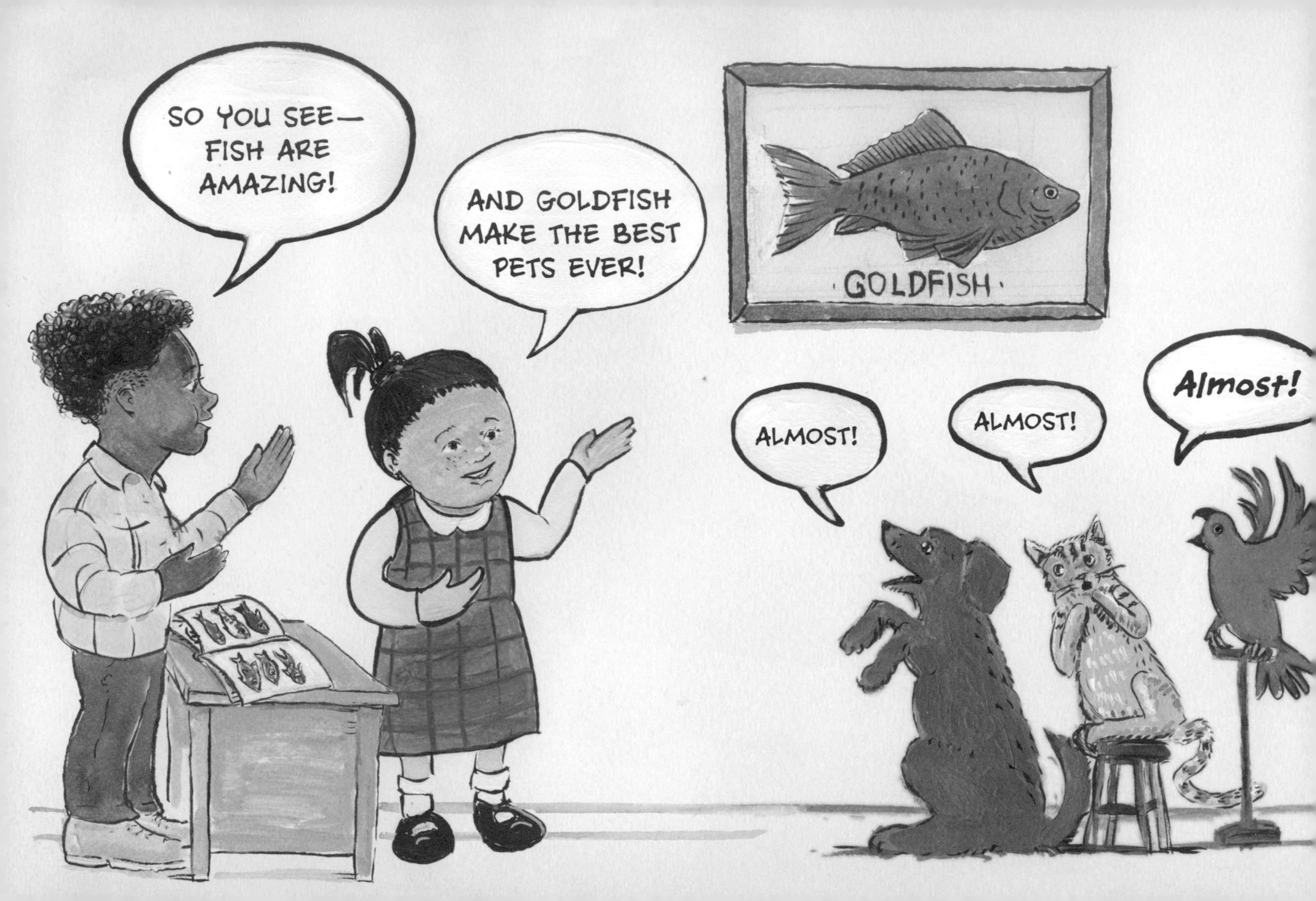
SO YOU SEE—
FISH ARE
AMAZING!
AND GOLDFISH
MAKE THE BEST
PETS EVER!
GOLDFISH
ALMOST!
ALMOST!
Almost!

ABOUT THE AUTHOR

Kevin McCloskey is the author of the critically acclaimed TOON Books *Giggle and Learn* series, which also includes *The Real Poop on Pigeons!* and *We Dig Worms!* He teaches illustration at Kutztown University, in Pennsylvania. Kevin says he discovered many things about goldfish thanks to his son, Daniel. "When he was a teenager, Daniel dug a small pond about the size of a bathrub. It was soon covered with water lillies," Kevin remembers. "Every winter the pond freezes over, but when spring comes, the fish are still alive. You see them when the ice becomes clear, all lined up next to the pump. I find that amazing. Neighborhood kids have brought us the fish they won at fairs. It's been almost twenty years and we now have about seventeen fish." Kevin adds, "I should point out that the various fish in this book would not all live in the same places. Some are deep-sea fish, and some are freshwater fish. I'm no scientist, but I love to learn by observing little creatures, especially those who live in my own backyard."

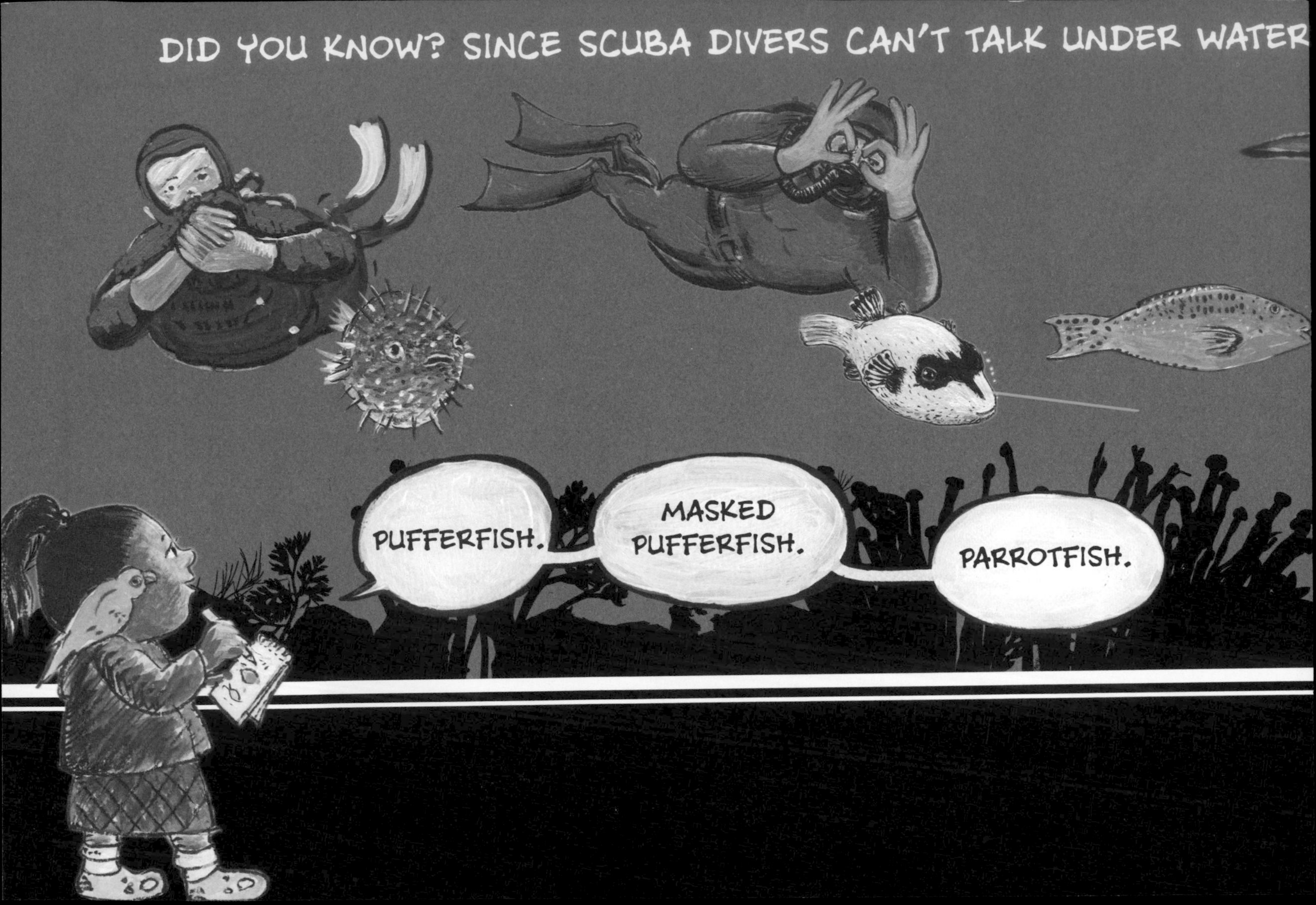
DID YOU KNOW? SINCE SCUBA DIVERS CAN'T TALK UNDER WATER
PUFFERFISH.
MASKED PUFFERFISH.
PARROTFISH.

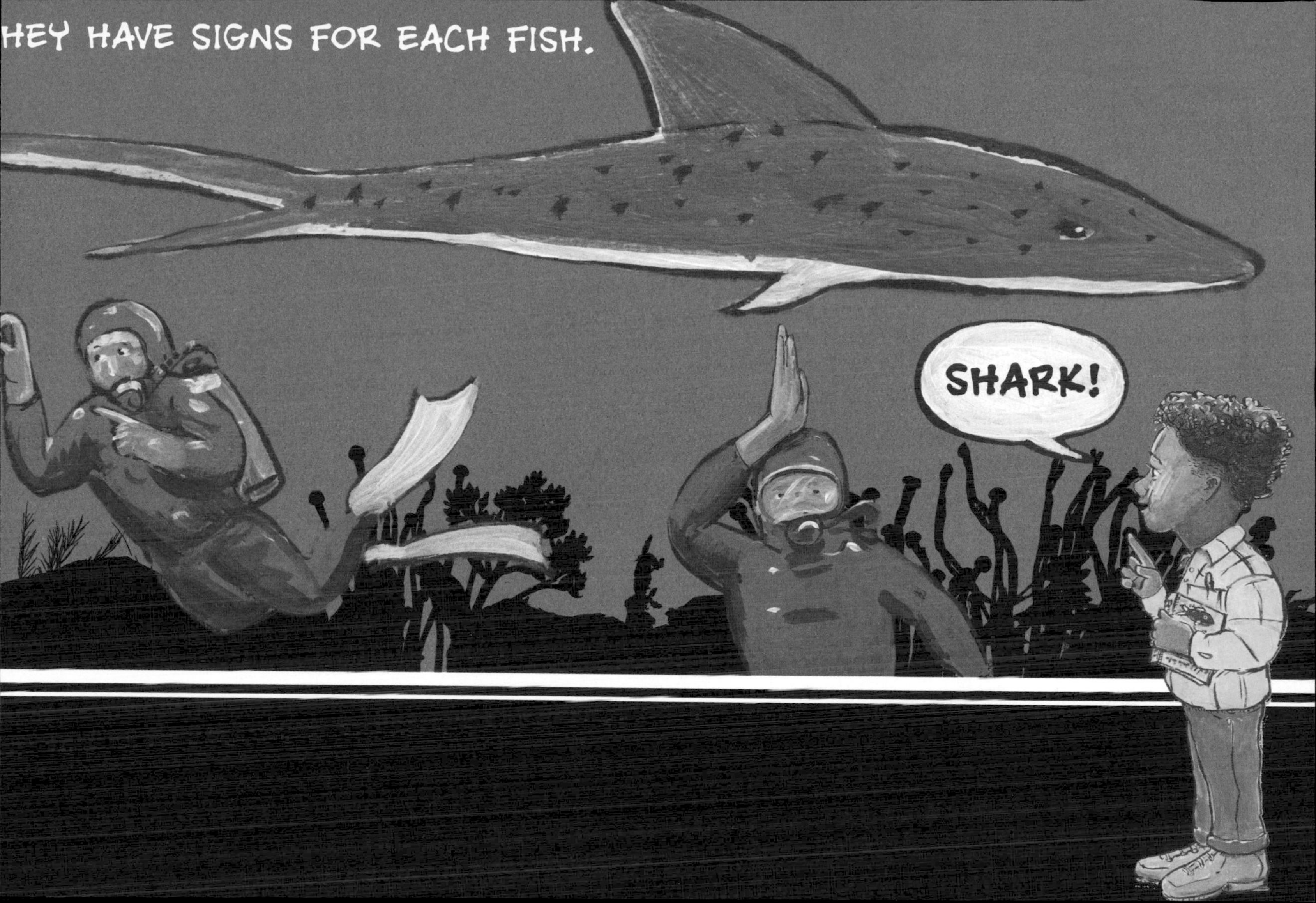
HEY HAVE SIGNS FOR EACH FISH.
SHARK!

TIPS FOR PARENTS AND TEACHERS:

HOW TO READ COMICS WITH KIDS

Kids love comics! They are naturally drawn to the details in the pictures, which make them want to read the words. Comics beg for repeated readings and let both emerging and reluctant readers enjoy complex stories with a rich vocabulary. But since comics have their own grammar, here are a few tips for reading them with kids:

GUIDE YOUNG READERS: Use your finger to show your place in the text, but keep it at the bottom of the character speaking so it doesn't hide the very important facial expressions.

HAM IT UP! Think of the comic book story as a play, and don't hesitate to read with expression and intonation. Assign parts or get kids to supply the sound effects, a great way to reinforce phonics skills.

LET THEM GUESS: Comics provide lots of context for the words, so emerging readers can make informed guesses. Like jigsaw puzzles, comics ask readers to make connections, so check children's understanding by asking "What's this character thinking?" (but don't be surprised if a kid finds some of the comics' subtle details faster than you).

TALK ABOUT THE PICTURES: Point out how the artist paces the story with pauses (silent panels) or speeded-up action (a burst of short panels). Discuss how the size and shape of the panels convey meaning.

ABOVE ALL, ENJOY! There is of course never one right way to read, so go for the shared pleasure. Once children make the story happen in their imagination, they have discovered the thrill of reading, and you won't be able to stop them. At that point, just go get them more books, and more comics.

www.TOON-BOOKS.com

SEE OUR FREE ONLINE CARTOON MAKERS, LESSON PLANS, AND MUCH MORE